# The Bible and the Christian Life

## Leland G. Shultz

Radiant BOOKS
Gospel Publishing House/Springfield, Mo. 65802

02-0857

© 1984 by the Gospel Publishing House, Springfield, Missouri 65802. All rights reserved. No part of this book may be reproduced, stored in a retrieval system, or transmitted in any form or by any means—electronic, mechanical, photocopy, recording, or otherwise—without prior written permission of the copyright owner, except brief quotations used in connection with reviews in magazines or newspapers.

Library of Congress Catalog Card Number 82-82701
International Standard Book Number 0-88243-857-3
Printed in the United States of America

A teacher's guide for individual or group study with this book is available from the Gospel Publishing House (order number 32-0198; ISBN 0-88243-198-6).

## *Contents*

1. The Bible—God's Word  5
2. The Bible Proved by Prophecy  14
3. The Bible's Theme—Christ  22
4. History's Greatest Event  31
5. All Men Are Sinners  40
6. Salvation  48
7. How To Be Saved  55
8. How To Live Victoriously  63
9. Walking in the Spirit  71
10. To Show the Lord's Death (Communion and Baptism)  80
11. Lord, Teach Us To Pray  89
12. Giving to God  97
13. Obedience  105

# 1
## *The Bible—God's Word*

All Scripture is given by inspiration of God, and is profitable for doctrine, for reproof, for correction, for instruction in righteousness (2 Timothy 3:16).

Waving a Bible in his hand a high school teacher asked his class, "Do you suppose this book is true?" He then put the Bible back on his desk, where it had been each day in obvious view of all of his students. He made no further comments. The question had been interjected into the middle of a totally unrelated subject.

This was only the beginning of a well-thought-out plan. There were many more interrupted lessons with other questions, each of them skillfully designed to plant seeds of doubt, to discredit the Bible, in the minds of the students.

Never were further statements made about the Bible, only questions—questions that were never discussed or answered; questions that left young minds confused, disillusioned, and filled with doubt.

This plan is neither new nor original. It is, in fact, as old as the sacred record itself. It was the very first attack ever used against the Word of God. The tempter in the Garden of Eden said to Eve, "Hath God said . . .?" (See Genesis 3:1.)

## "Hath God Said . . . ?"

That is the big question facing us today, "Hath God said . . . ?"

The question is just as important to us as it was to Eve. The same tempter is still suggesting that God surely didn't say all that is in the Bible.

Due to the media discovery of born-again Christians in the past few years, the evangelical world has a new image today. It is no longer unusual to hear or see news reports that include references to "born-again" people. This has not gone unnoticed by the unbelieving, secular, humanistic sector of society. They have often retaliated with slanders and innuendos about the "Bible-thumping, hell-fire evangelicals."

The fact that the secular humanist movement issued a 1980 declaration reiterating their anti-God philosophical position indicates their concern. Other less radical liberals have also joined their chorus. They know they cannot eradicate Christianity; all they want to do is to moderate Evangelicalism.

A whirlpool of controversy surrounds the inerrancy of the Bible. It has been instigated from without and within the church. Once again the question is being asked, "Hath God said . . . ?" The liberals do not deny the Bible; they ask whether the Bible is fully or partially trustworthy. In fact, they embrace and propagate the view that the Bible *contains* the Word of God, but the Bible is not necessarily *the* Word of God. Is the Bible then partly true and partly false?

This liberal view says, "Yes, God hath spoken, but so has man. Some of the Bible is divine and some is human." This, of course, makes it necessary that someone be established to help define which parts of the Bible are true and which are untrue.

## God Hath Said!

It is interesting that while the tempter faced Eve with the question, "Hath God said . . . ?" she immediately responded with the truth, "Yea, God hath said!" That is our answer to the critics today. God has said! The Bible is God's Word. The accepted Christian view of the Bible is that it is God's Word. God spoke through holy men He chose to use. The entire Bible is true, and it is the only true and dependable authority for Christian faith and conduct.

Too often books, lectures, and sermons are punctuated with "according to the latest scholars," "it is the opinion of . . . ," "some of the best minds on this subject say . . . ," or "in my opinion. . . . " What is needed is more proclaiming of "Thus saith the Lord . . . ," "It is written . . . , " and "God hath said . . . !"

## Mistakes of Moses?

Moses was one of the instruments God chose to use to speak to the Children of Israel and all of mankind. But God had to do the unusual to get Moses' attention. He caused a bush to burn without being consumed. Out of that bush God called Moses to lead the Children of Israel and to bring His message to them. Moses objected. Because Moses stuttered and stammered, he told God He was mistaken. But God was not looking for eloquence, only a usable servant. Moses became that servant.

Some people talk about "the mistakes of Moses," referring especially to the accounts of Creation, the Flood, the miraculous crossing of the Red Sea, and the plagues of Egypt. They also mention the Books of Moses, Genesis through Deuteronomy, which they suppose are filled with legends and are survivals of primitive religious thinking.

The Books of Moses have probably been attacked more than any other portion of the Bible. They have been said to be historically incorrect, scientifically inaccurate, and untrue.

Although the Bible was not written as a textbook on medicine, mathematics, chemistry, or philosophy, when it addresses these subjects, it is true. In fact, the Bible has enlightened men to more clearly understand some of these subjects.

In Exodus 17:14 we are told how Moses wrote these Books: "And the Lord said unto Moses, Write this for a memorial in a book."

> And Moses came and told the people all the words of the Lord, and all the judgments: and all the people answered with one voice, and said, All the words which the Lord hath said will we do. And Moses wrote all the words of the Lord (Exodus 24:3,4).

Moses was so convinced that he had written what the Lord wanted and intended that he declared:

> Ye shall not add unto the word which I command you, neither shall ye diminish aught from it, that ye may keep the commandments of the Lord your God which I command you (Deuteronomy 4:2).

Moses knew the laws and traditions of Egypt and Babylon. His knowledge might well have influenced his leadership. But over and over again, from the first chapter to the last, Moses declared that God had spoken to him. Thirty-eight times he repeated, "And the Lord called unto Moses . . . speak unto the children of Israel," and twelve more times he said this in slightly different words. Moses was guided by God in establishing the Levitical system. No wonder it reflects a wisdom far beyond anything else in ancient legislation.

Mistakes of Moses? Hardly.

And so no one would forget where this great system came from, Moses concluded the book with these words: "These are the commandments which the Lord commanded Moses for the children of Israel in mount Sinai" (Leviticus 27:34).

## Mouthpieces

Some of the men God used to speak to Israel were called prophets. "God . . . spake in time past . . . by the prophets" (Hebrews 1:1). The prophets were not just predictors of future events. God spoke to them and through them. A prophet is also a forth-teller, a spokesman, a mouthpiece, one who speaks for another. The prophetic formula was "Thus saith Jehovah."

The great prophet Isaiah began the account of his testimony by declaring, "Hear, O heavens, and give ear, O earth: for the Lord hath spoken" (Isaiah 1:2). For 62 years Isaiah's messages were continual reminders that he was speaking the word of the Lord. He closed his messages by beginning the last chapter of Isaiah with "Thus saith the Lord" (Isaiah 66:1).

Jeremiah was God's spokesman in days of darkness and disaster. In establishing his mission Jeremiah said, "Then the word of the Lord came unto me, saying . . ." (Jeremiah 1:4). Over and over again he said, "Moreover the word of the Lord came unto me . . . ," or "The Lord showed me . . . ," or "Thus saith the Lord . . . ." He left no question in anyone's mind that he was God's spokesman.

Ezekiel's messages were often expressed by the use of symbols, like the two sticks he wrote on and the boiling pot filled with bones. But more often he was given messages through visions. Perhaps the most well-known vision is described in an old spiritual song: "Ezekiel saw the wheel, way up in the middle of the air. The big wheel it run by faith, and the little wheel run by the grace of God."

And there were other prophets—some well-known and some not so well-known—like Daniel, David, Amos, Hosea, Obadiah, and more. All of these men fully believed they were communicating the words of God.

## A Miracle

Almost anyone could tell you the Bible is a book of miracles, from beginning to end. Perhaps one of the greatest miracles of all is the Bible itself.

Only a multitude of miracles could have given us the Bible. The Word of God has come down to us in written form so that all men and every generation can read what God has to say.

What are the chances of the Bible being written, preserved, and handed down to mankind as it has been? Thirty different authors, many of whom lived generations apart, wrote the 66 books of the Bible during a period of 1600 years. They were men of different languages, cultures, and occupations, yet they wrote under the inspiration of God. In the Bible we find an absolute unity of vision, structure, message, and doctrine.

This unity is not superficial. In fact, throughout the centuries critics have done their best to discredit the Bible. However, the deeper they have probed, the more obvious the unity of the Word has become. Thousands of archaeologists, professional and amateur, have dug into ancient ruins throughout the land of the Bible. The relics they have unearthed only validate the accuracy and unity of the Bible—God's Word.

## Cover to Cover

The apostle Paul faced a hostile situation when he was brought before Governor Felix. His accusers charged him with being a troublemaker, an agitator, a source of disturbance, and a ringleader of the sect of the Nazarenes.

When he was finally given an opportunity to speak in his own defense, Paul cut right to the heart of their ugly feelings. He told them they couldn't prove anything they had accused him of. But Paul said he worshiped the God of his fathers and he believed "all things which are written in the law and in the prophets" (Acts 24:14). The only heresy the Jews could rightly charge him with was that he believed "all." They did not believe all the Scriptures. This was, in fact, the rebuke Jesus gave the Jews who were seeking to kill Him: "But if ye believe not his [Moses] writings, how shall ye believe my words?" (John 5:47).

The words of Paul in the text of this chapter say it a bit more formally: "All Scripture is given by inspiration of God, and is profitable for doctrine, for reproof, for correction, for instruction in righteousness" (2 Timothy 3:16).

Theologians have quibbled over this Scripture passage. Some want it to mean "all Scripture is inspired," while others contend for "all inspired Scriptures," thus implying that some Scripture passages are not inspired.

The original text allows the use of our English words *all* or *every*. In any case, Paul is emphasizing the fact that the Christian faith is guaranteed by its inspired Scriptures.

As you read through the writings of Paul, you become aware that he accepted the Scriptures as inspired of God. He was not discussing a theory of inspiration when he said, "All Scripture is given by inspiration of God"; he was simply stating a fact. From his youth Timothy had been taught the Scriptures; Paul did not need to assure him that they were inspired. The thrust of Paul's words was that the Scriptures are profitable. He was emphasizing to Timothy that for a Christian to be completely "furnished," the Scriptures must continually be applied to life. The Christian life must be centered on the Word.

The Scriptures are profitable for teaching and learning doctrine. There is no other reliable source. All doctrines, theories, theologies, and ethics must be held up to the light of the Word, not to find fault, but to expose false teaching and dangers in Christian conduct.

Correction is too often considered to be negative. It is associated with discipline for doing wrong. However, correction is also a positive action. Consider how an automobile is driven. It is guided by a continuous series of corrective actions. Each movement of the steering wheel corrects the direction of the car to keep it on the road. If you wait too long to correct the direction, you may end up off the road and in a ditch.

The application of the Bible to daily life has the same effect. That's why the Scriptures need to be read regularly. Each day they will shed light that will help us steer our lives in the right direction.

The Word is also for instruction in righteousness. That sounds so ecclesiastical, almost "holier-than-thou." In its simplest definition, however, righteousness means rightness, right conduct, right living.

Today's world system would have us believe that it's impossible to know what is right. Everything is relative, so what is right to one person is not right to another. There are no absolutes.

Jean-Paul Sartre, an existential atheist, declared that since there is no God, there are no normative values to which we can appeal; there is neither good nor evil; there is no morality that can prescribe one kind of behavior rather than another.

Solomon described this worldly philosophy when he said, "There is a way that seemeth right unto a man; but the end thereof are the ways of death" (Proverbs 16:25).

# 2

## *The Bible Proved by Prophecy*

There is a God in heaven that revealeth secrets (Daniel 2:28).

Man is obsessed with an insatiable desire for knowing the future. People are fascinated with the unknown. The untiring search has employed divination, telepathy, dreams, apparitions, witchcraft, astrology, horoscopes, and many other aberrations.

Jeane Dixon, reigning queen of the occult, boasts some remarkable fulfillments of some of her predictions. The record shows that she accurately predicted the assassination of President John F. Kennedy in 1963. However, she blundered in her prediction that World War III would begin in 1958.

On nearly every continent overzealous people have claimed special revelations of the future. Some of them set dates and times for events to happen. But when "doomsday" arrived, nothing happened.

The future is God's, and it will be written God's way. The authority to perceive it has not been given to cults, religions, or the media. God alone is the custodian of the future. Outside of divine illumination, the best that man can do is to "see through a glass, darkly" (1 Corinthians 13:12).

## The Age of Aquarius?

A few years ago a rock song asserting, "This is the dawning of Aquarius," gained almost instant popularity. Some believed this was the advent of the age of astrology. But astrology had been with us for many years already.

Ancient Babylon was the seat of sorcery, the spawning pool of the occult world. The Chaldeans were addicted to the study of the stars. The Babylonians built huge pyramid-shaped buildings they called ziggurats. These housed their temples. From their balconies the astrologers charted the courses of the stars. The tower of Babylon was believed to have been one of their tallest ziggurats. Their gods and goddesses were legion.

Nebuchadnezzar, king of Babylon, selected the wisest and best of the Chaldean magicians, astrologers, and sorcerers to compose a special king's cabinet. When he invaded Jerusalem he took hostages of the Jews. These were to be the choicest of young men—men of wisdom and knowledge. He added these young men to his cabinet of confidants. Daniel was one of the hostages. His name was changed to Belteshazzar, which means "Bel's Prince." Bel was the national god of the Babylonians. This special inner circle received preferential treatment. They ate the king's meat and drank his wine.

## The Illusive Dream

Suddenly everything changed. The king decreed a mass execution of the wise men, unless they could tell him exactly what he wanted to know. He had awakened from a terribly frightening dream—a dream he could not recall. The details were gone, and the fear of not knowing them haunted him. He could not go back to sleep. "My spirit is troubled to know the dream," he cried. Early in the morning he called for the wise men and demanded they tell him both the dream and its meaning.

The magicians tried their charms, repeated their incantations, but failed to receive the dream or its interpretation. The sorcerers prepared their potions and magical drugs, but no dream came. The astrologers applied their various divinations and enchantments, but they too failed. The wise men could not tell the king his dream or its meaning.

In desperation they told the king he was asking the impossible. They said, "There is not a man upon the earth that can show the king's matter" (Daniel 2:10).

The intensity of the king's troubled spirit demanded their immediate death. He ordered the wise men to be cut into pieces and their homes destroyed.

The executioners gathered the men to carry out the king's order. As they approached Daniel, he asked what it was all about. For some reason he had not been summoned to the meeting with the king. Perhaps someone had thought this young Jewish boy was inadequate. As he stood before the troubled king, Daniel reminded him how the other wise men had failed. "But," he said, "there is a God in heaven that revealeth secrets, and maketh known . . . what shall be in the latter days" (Daniel 2:28).

## The Revealer of Secrets

Daniel drove his point home: All of your gods have been tried. Your wise men study the heavens. They chart the stars and make interpretations. But only one God, the God of the heavens, reveals secrets.

The prophet's message has never been more appropriate than it is today. Hundreds of newspapers carry syndicated columns by some of the modern-day seers. Jeane Dixon's predictions are among them. According to a 12-month analysis of her predictions, she was right about 60 percent of the time. The Bible is accurate 100 percent of the time.

No other sacred book or any other religion anywhere in the world contains such accurate prophecy or predictions of future events. God's Word, the Bible, stands alone as the source book of reliable prophecy.

"Holy men of God spake as they were moved by the Holy Ghost" (2 Peter 1:21). Other writers could record history and document genealogies of nations. Others could preserve the intricate and intimate details of religious celebrations. And others could chronicle wars and records of civilizations. But only God could make predictions hundreds of years ahead of events and have history record their fulfillment to the minutest details.

When Daniel stood before the king to make known the dream and its interpretation, he prefaced his remarks with: "This secret is not revealed to me for any wisdom that I have more than any living" (Daniel 2:30). He wanted to make sure to give God the credit. God had revealed the dream and its interpretation when Daniel and his friends prayed.

God's prophets were trustworthy by their prophecies and their lives.

## The Big Image

The king saw a big image that frightened him. How big, we don't know. Some translators of the Hebrew use words like "gigantic," "colossal," and "extraordinarily large." We know that Nebuchadnezzar made an image of gold that was 90 feet tall. Maybe it was as large as the Statue of Liberty, 151 feet high. There were many large images throughout Babylon, so this one must have dwarfed the others. We do know this: The king was awed.

Perhaps some of the awesomeness was in the appearance of the statue: "whose brightness was excellent" (Daniel 2:31). One writer believes the context of the words indicates the beholder was dazzled by the shimmering brilliance of the statue's polished metal surface.

There was a third reason for the king to be so deeply impressed. Unlike any other likeness of a man he had seen, this one had five distinct parts. The head of the image was fashioned in "fine gold." No wonder it shone with such magnificence. The chest and arms were of shining silver. The belly and thighs were polished brass. The legs of the image were of iron, and the feet of iron and clay.

There was a fourth reason for the king to be impressed, and probably distressed. Babylon was filled with images. Images were built of most of the gods and goddesses of the Babylonians. The king might have been impressed because this image superseded anything in his land. But as he looked at the image in its dazzling beauty, something awful happened. A huge boulder crashed onto the feet of the magnificent image. The lifeless giant crashed to the ground. It not only broke into pieces, but it also disintegrated and spread across the land like a cloud of volcanic ash. The boulder began to grow. Like a bulging lava dome of a volcano it grew and grew until it filled all the earth. That was his dream. No wonder Nebuchadnezzar was terrified!

### The Interpretation

Daniel described the dream in detail. No doubt as he began to recall it for Nebuchadnezzar the whole dream resurfaced in his mind. "Tell me the interpretation" was the second of his demands. "Why was the majestic image destroyed?"

The great image was a concrete symbol of world kingdoms. Daniel explained the interpretation to the king, "Thou art this head of gold" (Daniel 2:38). Nebuchadnezzar's reign was certainly the golden age. The gold of the temple had been only one source of his plunder. Rife with golden images, Babylon was a city of splendor.

The breast and arms of the image were silver, representing the kingdom of Medo-Persia. Silver, being less precious than gold, denoted a rule and a prosperity inferior to the preceding empire.

A third kingdom was depicted by the brass belly and thighs of the image. The Grecian Empire led by Alexander the Great was the age of bronze. It was a kingdom that began unified and strong, but ended divided, as depicted by the thighs.

While the symbolism of metal from one kingdom to another showed deterioration, it also represented an increase in strength. The legs of the image were of the strongest metal of all, iron. They portrayed the mighty Roman Empire, which, as Daniel said, would "break in pieces and bruise" (Daniel 2:40). This great empire did exactly that. Nations succumbed to her supremacy, but in time Rome was divided. Her strength was diminished as she was split into eastern and western divisions.

The feet and toes of the image were made of iron and clay—two incompatible elements. Daniel saw a strange mixture of governments, "partly strong, and partly broken" (Daniel 2:42). The 10 toes represented 10 kingdoms, kingdoms having their origins in the nations that formerly comprised the entire image. These nations mingle but have no cohesiveness among them. They will be brought together in a coalition of 10 nations.

This coalition is in the making. The 10 toes are in the process of formation. There is an alignment of the European Economic Community. Emerging from that amalgamation of iron and clay could come the Antichrist and the final conflagration.

## The Rock of Ages

The momentous end-time events of the world will soon bring in the Rock of Ages! In the king's dream "a stone was cut out without hands, . . . and broke them [the feet of the image] in pieces. . . . And the stone that struck the image became a great mountain and filled the whole earth" (Daniel 2:34, 35, NKJV).

In both the Old and New Testaments, *rock* can be found to symbolize Jesus, the Son of God.

In referring to the rock that went with the Children of Israel through the wilderness wandering, and that poured forth streams of living water, Paul says, "That Rock was Christ" (1 Corinthians 10:4).

Christ was also the Psalmist's "Rock in a weary land."

Jesus said, "Upon this rock I will build my church; and the gates of hell shall not prevail against it" (Matthew 16:18). What rock is this? "No other foundation than that which is [already] laid, . . . Jesus Christ" (1 Corinthians 3:11, NKJV). He is the Rock for all time.

Peter too had something to say about the Rock of Ages: "a living stone, disallowed indeed of men, but chosen of God, and precious" (1 Peter 2:4). And then he includes God's children in on the "Stone Age":

> Ye also, as lively stones, are built up a spiritual house, a holy priesthood, to offer up spiritual sacrifices, acceptable to God by Jesus Christ. . . . Unto you therefore which believe he is precious: but unto them which be disobedient, the stone which the builders disallowed, the same is made the head of the corner, and a stone of stumbling, and a rock of offense (1 Peter 2:5,7,8).

The kingdoms of this world will become God's kingdom. This Kingdom shall never pass away. It will consume all others and will stand forever.

And in the days of these kings [the 10 toes] shall the God of heaven set up a kingdom, which shall never be destroyed: and the kingdom shall not be left to other people (Daniel 2:44).

The prophecies in the second chapter of Daniel have been fulfilled, are being fulfilled, and will be fulfilled. They are one of the greatest examples of prophecy and fulfillment in the Bible. They reach back into ancient history and spill out onto the front pages of today's newspapers.

What are the chances of the fulfillment of these prophecies just happening?

There is a mathematical formula for determining the likelihood of predictions. The formula has two parts: simple and compound probability. Compound probability is applied to any prediction of more than one detail. Any prediction with two probabilities has one chance in four of fulfillment. Each probability that is added makes the possibility of fulfillment less likely. The odds of the many details of prophecy in the second chapter of Daniel being fulfilled are staggering. Chance or coincidence is out of the question.

Dr. C. I. Scofield writes:

> Fulfilled prophecy is a proof of inspiration because the Scriptures' predictions of future events were uttered so long before the events transpired that no merely human sagacity or foresight could have anticipated them, and these predictions are so detailed, minute, and specific as to exclude the possibility that they were fortunate guesses. It is certain, therefore, the Scriptures which contain them are inspired.

"Prophecy came not in old time by the will of man: but holy men of God spake as they were moved by the Holy Ghost" (2 Peter 1:21).

# 3
## The Bible's Theme—Christ

> Search the Scriptures; . . . they testify of me (John 5:39).

In December 1968, Apollo VIII was launched from John F. Kennedy Space Center at Merritt Island, Florida, on a lunar mission. On the second revolution around the earth, the astronauts were given the signal from Mission Control, "Go for TLI [translunar injection]."

Astronaut Frank Borman maneuvered the spacecraft into firing position and the third rocket stage thrust the crew at more than 24,000 miles an hour toward the moon. During the flight the crew aimed portable television cameras at the earth.

On December 24, the astronauts spent the day orbiting the moon and photographing the moon's surface and a three-quarters earth. The pictures showed a bluish earth against a black sky, and the crater-pocked moon surface in the foreground. On Christmas Eve, while TV cameras televised close-up views of the moon, the crew gazed out their windows at the earth, as they read Genesis 1:1-10 to earthlings.

The past and the present were never more beautifully brought together than at that moment. Mankind was enjoying one of its greatest triumphs. Scientific technology had sent men on an incredible journey to the moon, while millions of people watched on their television sets. It was a humbling moment when Frank Borman's voice was heard reading, "In the beginning God created the heaven and the earth."

God intended the earth to be as beautiful and as tranquil as it appeared to the astronauts who viewed it from so far away. In the beginning, He prepared a beautiful garden called Eden. It was the fairest spot in the newly made world. This garden was not merely a place of residence; it was intended to afford Adam and Eve sweet gratification, wholesome and pleasurable enjoyment. It was a paradise. In fact, its very name means "pleasure," "delight."

## Paradise Lost

The beauty and serenity of paradise was soon marred. Adam and Eve succumbed to the tempter. The encounter between Eve and the serpent began a struggle that has continued throughout the ages. We cannot begin to imagine the enormity of the conflict.

Adam and Eve were surrounded by bountiful provisions. In Eden they could enjoy one another, eat of the fruit of the trees, and walk and talk with God. But then they disobeyed Him. And the beauty was gone. The peace they had known was displaced by fear. Their unmarked consciences were suddenly pointing accusing fingers at them. Now upon seeing their nakedness they were ashamed.

Their feeble attempt at hiding behind self-made aprons of fig leaves was symbolic of the entire episode. The conflict was essentially between right and wrong, between light and darkness, between Satan and God. Paradise was lost. Adam and Eve were still in the Garden, but it wasn't the same. As a matter of fact, nothing would ever be the same again. Their relationship had changed. Their nearness to God had been forfeited.

God could not tolerate willful disobedience. He would have to evict them from Eden. The first recorded conversation between God and man was God calling out in the Garden to Adam, "Where art thou?" (Genesis 3:9). God knew, but He wanted them to admit their guilt. And they did—by hiding in fear!

The ensuing picture is not pleasant. God drove Adam and Eve out of the Garden of Eden (Genesis 3:24). The gate was shut, barred by an angel with a flaming sword. The break between God and the crown of His creation was complete.

## Farewell Gifts of Fur Coats

It was not without pain that God closed the gate to Eden. He cared greatly for His creation. Before sending Adam and Eve away, He made "coats of skins, and clothed them" (Genesis 3:21). The clothes were more than coverings for their bodies. The coats were furnished from the hides of animals. For the first time animals were slain, blood was shed, to make a covering for man. This was the beginning of a great and glorious plan of God for covering all the sins of mankind.

## In the Beginning—Jesus

A story line was established that flows throughout the Bible. It is Jesus. God had a plan for man's redemption, and in Genesis, the first book of the Bible, the book of beginnings, God gives us a glimpse of this plan. The first promise of a Redeemer is wrapped up in God's words to the serpent: "It shall bruise thy head, and thou shalt bruise his heel" (Genesis 3:15). The seed of the woman will ultimately triumph.

Here is another amazing proof of the authenticity of

the Bible. Every writer in every book of the Bible portrays Jesus Christ in some way. In some instances He is spoken of prophetically, in other instances He is shadowed in types and Levitical institutions. But He is always there. Jesus is so intrinsically woven into the Word that we find Him everywhere.

## Search the Scriptures

Jesus said, "Search the Scriptures; . . . they . . . testify of me" (John 5:39). The Bible is not to be worshiped; it is to be studied. The world needs the Bible because the world needs Jesus, and Jesus can be found in the Bible.

I grew up in a church where I sat under the ministry of good pastors. They were men of the Word. Listening to their sermons as a boy, I was intrigued. It seemed that no matter which book they selected sermon texts from—Genesis, Psalms, or Revelation—they always ended up preaching about Jesus. In my youth I saw only Moses, Abraham, David, or Paul in the texts of those preachers. But they had "searched the Scriptures"; they recognized Jesus in the shadows, types, and prophecies.

Jesus is the theme of the Bible from the first book to the last. "In the beginning was the Word, and the Word was with God, and the Word was God" (John 1:1).

Jesus was there right from the beginning (see Genesis 1:26).

Changing the metaphor, John the Baptist said, "Behold the *Lamb* of God, which taketh away the sin of the world!" (John 1:29).

Look again at the picture in the Garden of Eden. There is the metaphor of the Lamb in the slain animal and coats of skins. There is the *wounded* Lamb, the heel bruised by the serpent.

The Lamb is also typified in the sacrifice made by Abel as he brought the firstlings of his flock.

One of the most moving stories in the Old Testament is the story of Abraham's offer of his son Isaac on an altar of sacrifice. Maybe I can feel the pathos because I am the father of two sons. It had to be agonizing for Abraham. Perhaps even more so when Isaac said to him, "Behold the fire and the wood: but where is the lamb for a burnt offering? And Abraham said, My son, God will provide himself a lamb for a burnt offering" (Genesis 22:7,8). God will provide—and He did. Just before Abraham brought the knife down to slay his son, God provided a ram for the sacrifice.

The *Lamb* of God is seen again in Exodus. The Children of Israel were told to slay a lamb without blemish, and apply the blood to the lintel and side posts of the door. No one fulfills this type of the slain lamb and shed blood except Jesus Christ.

Philip, the evangelist, told of hearing an important Ethiopian dignitary sitting in his chariot reading from Isaiah the prophet: "The place of the Scripture which he read was this, He was led as a sheep to the slaughter; and like a lamb dumb before his shearer, so opened he not his mouth" (Acts 8:32). Since the man did not understand what he read, Philip joined him and "began at the same Scripture, and preached unto him Jesus" (Acts 8:35). Once again Jesus is identified as the *Lamb* of God, foretold by the prophet Isaiah.

### Lion—Lamb

John, the revelator, gives us another magnificent view of Jesus Christ, the *Lamb* of God, in the fifth chapter of Revelation. No other scene can match this one for its majesty. John's vision was of the throne in the high court of heaven. The eternal Father sat in the supreme seat of authority, and in His right hand He held a sealed book. John wept because no one could be found in heaven or on earth worthy to open the book. Then one of the elders said, "Weep not: behold, the Lion of the tribe of Judah, the Root of David, hath prevailed to open the book, and to loose the seven seals thereof. And I beheld, . . . in the midst of the elders, stood a Lamb" (Revelation 5:5,6).

No man, in any age, at any place in the entire world has ever witnessed such a scene as that which took place when the *Lamb* took the book from the Father. It staggers the mind to imagine what it must have looked and sounded like. The 24 elders around the throne began to sing, 'Thou art worthy to take the book, . . . for thou wast slain, and hast redeemed us to God by thy blood out of every kindred, and tongue, and people, and nation" (Revelation 5:9).

## Legions of Angels Honor the Lamb

And suddenly they all were surrounded by more than 100 million angels singing, "Worthy is the *Lamb* that was slain to receive power, and riches, and wisdom, and strength, and honor, and glory, and blessing" (Revelation 5:12).

The grand finale came when the angels were joined by every creature, in heaven, on earth, under the earth, and in the sea, saying: "Blessing, and honor, and glory, and power, be unto him that sitteth upon the throne, and unto the *Lamb* for ever and ever" (Revelation 5:13). Hallelujah! Praise the Lord (the Lamb)!

"Search the Scriptures; . . . they . . . testify of me" (John 5:39). Indeed, they do! Jesus' portrait is found in every book of the Bible:

In Genesis He is the Seed of the woman.

In Exodus He is the Passover Lamb.

In Leviticus He is our High Priest.

In Numbers He is the Pillar of Cloud.

In Deuteronomy He is the Prophet like unto Moses.

In Joshua He is the Captain of our salvation.

In Judges He is our Judge and Lawgiver.

In Ruth He is our Kinsman–Redeemer.

In 1 and 2 Samuel He is our Trusted Prophet.

In Kings and Chronicles He is our Reigning King.

In Ezra He is our Faithful Scribe.

In Nehemiah He is the Rebuilder of the broken-down wall of human life.

In Esther He is our Mordecai.

In Job He is our Ever-living Redeemer.

In Psalms He is our Shepherd.

In Proverbs and Ecclesiastes He is our Wisdom.

In the Song of Solomon He is our Lover and Bridegroom.

In Isaiah He is the Prince of Peace.

In Jeremiah He is the Righteous Branch.

In Lamentations He is our Weeping Prophet.

In Ezekiel He is the Wonderful four-faced Man.

In Daniel He is the Fourth Man in life's fiery furnace.

In Hosea He is the Faithful Husband—forever married to the backslider.

In Joel He is the Baptizer with the Holy Ghost and Fire.

In Amos He is our Burden Bearer.

In Obadiah He is the Mighty to Save.

In Jonah He is our great Foreign Missionary.

In Micah He is the Messenger of Beautiful Feet.

In Nahum He is the Avenger of God's Elect.

In Habakkuk He is God's Evangelist saying, "Revive the work in the midst of the years."

In Zephaniah He is our Saviour.

In Haggai He is the Restorer of God's Lost Heritage.

In Zechariah He is the Fountain opened in the House of David for sin and uncleanness.

In Malachi He is the Sun of righteousness, rising with healing in His wings.

In Matthew He is the Messiah.

In Mark He is the Wonder-worker.

In Luke He is the Son of Man.

In John He is the Son of God.

In Acts He is the Holy Ghost.

In Romans He is our Justifier.

In 1 and 2 Corinthians He is the gifts of the Spirit.

In Galatians He is the Redeemer from the curse of the Law.

In Ephesians He is the Christ of unsearchable riches.

In Philippians He is the God who supplies all our needs.

In Colossians He is the Fullness of the Godhead bodily.

In 1 and 2 Thessalonians He is our soon-coming King.

In 1 and 2 Timothy He is our Mediator between God and man.

In Titus He is our faithful Pastor.

In Philemon He is the Friend that sticketh closer than a brother.

In Hebrews He is the Blood of the Everlasting Covenant.

In James He is our Great Physician, for the prayer of faith shall save the sick.

In 1 and 2 Peter He is our Chief Shepherd who soon shall appear with a crown of unfading glory.

In 1, 2, and 3 John He is Love.

In Jude He is the Lord coming with ten thousands of His saints.

In Revelation He is the King of Kings, Lord of Lords, and Alpha and Omega: "I am Alpha and Omega, the first and the last" (Revelation 1:11).

# 4

## *History's Greatest Event*

As in Adam all die, even so in Christ shall all be made alive (1 Corinthians 15:22).

The warm spring air was heavy with the aroma of fresh blossoms. We walked along a winding path between brilliantly colored flowers that led to a series of colorful ceramic murals on the garden wall. The scenes depicted events from the life of Christ: as a babe lying in the manger, as a boy inquiring in the temple, as a man stilling the sea. The artist had captured the emotion and pathos of the crucifixion: the crowd, the soldiers, the darkened sky. The path from that scene led to an exit from the garden.

I backtracked, looking for other scenes, but there were none. No tomb, no open grave, no signs of resurrection—only death. As my wife and I walked out of the garden, she sighed, "How sad!"

The disciples, family, and friends of Jesus must have felt the same when they actually saw Jesus hanging on the cross. No, not the same, their emotions were much, much deeper.

Everywhere Jesus went people crowded to hear Him, to see Him, or to be touched by His healing hand. His band of believers was growing. Becoming convinced that Jesus was the promised redeemer of Israel, more and more people were beginning to count on His kingdom being established.

Then suddenly everything they had hoped for and lived for was gone. All of those lofty and noble truths Jesus had taught them seemed to have died and been buried with Him in the sepulcher.

## Their Words Seemed Like Idle Tales

There is no evidence that anyone really believed Jesus would ever rise again. His enemies were satisfied they had solved their problem by doing away with Him. His followers were confused, disillusioned, and disappointed. Jesus had told them what to expect, but they did not understand.

Even the women, who seemed to be more perceptive, did not go to the tomb expecting it to be empty. They went to embalm His body. Mary was frightened by what she saw. She ran to tell the disciples, not that Jesus was risen, but that they had taken away His body, and she didn't know where (John 20:2).

When the disciples met, they were utterly disspirited. In fact, when Mary came to tell them she had seen the Lord, she found them mourning and weeping. When the disciples heard He was alive, they did not believe it. Two of them went to Emmaus, and on their way they talked of the tragedy that had befallen their group. They were sad as they commiserated with one another.

The chief priests and elders were astonished that Jesus was not in the tomb. To protect themselves, they bribed the soldiers, to whom had been committed the security of the tomb. They offered the soldiers large sums of money to perjure themselves by declaring, "His disciples . . . stole him away while we slept" (Matthew 28:13).

But, in spite of the disbelief among His followers, the dishonest maneuvering by the high priests, and the bitter anger of the crucifying crowd, Jesus broke the chains of death and came out of His grave alive!

## Only Jesus Could Say, I Lay Down My Life—
## I Take It Up Again

The world has witnessed many founders of religions, profound and superficial, significant and insignificant. Although some of these religions have stood the test of time, the founders themselves have not—they are dead.

Buddha is the title given to the teacher, founder, and leader of the Buddhist religion. Many stories present him as a divine being sent to earth in the form of a man. Buddha died about 483 B.C. at the age of 80. He experienced no resurrection, only death.

"There is no God but Allah, and Mohammed is his prophet." These are the first words of the prayer of the Moslems as they bow toward Mecca. But Mohammed died at age 61. While millions visit his tomb each year, he still lies buried.

Jesus Christ might have been listed among the "Who's Who" of religion had He remained in the tomb of Joseph of Arimathea.

I stood looking into the open door of the garden tomb in Jerusalem as I listened to the guide say, "This may have been the tomb. We don't know for sure. According to Biblical description it had to be at least in this general area, possibly within hundreds of yards of here, if not this very place."

The place of Christ's burial is not important; the fact of His resurrection is. His birth, life, teachings, and death have only historical significance without the Resurrection. The cross alone is bad news, an ignominious, tragic mistake. The Resurrection makes it good news. The Resurrection established Christ's claim to divinity, demonstrating His statement, "I lay down my life, that

33

I might take it again. No man taketh it from me, but I lay it down myself. . . . I have power to take it again" (John 10:17,18).

The church Jesus came to establish began to falter at His death. His disciples began reverting to their old occupations. This is epitomized by Peter: "I am going fishing! They said to him, 'We are going with you also' " (John 21:3, NKJV).

Not only was Jesus resurrected, His disciples were also "resurrected." All their hopes and dreams were revived. He opened their understanding and everything He had taught them began to take on a new meaning.

## Paul Declared the Good News—The Gospel

The apostle Paul dedicated the entire 15th chapter in his first epistle to the church at Corinth to the cardinal fact of the Christian faith: the Resurrection. He began by saying, "I declare unto you the gospel" (1 Corinthians 15:1). The gospel he declared was profoundly simple. First, Christ died for our sins according to the Scriptures; second, He was buried according to the Scriptures; and third, He rose again the third day according to the Scriptures.

Paul always stood on firm ground; his preaching was "according to the Scriptures." The Scriptures have a lot to say about the gospel, especially about the Resurrection. Wilbur Smith in *Therefore Stand* (New Canaan, CT: Keats Publishing Inc., 1981), says, "If you lifted out every passage in the New Testament in which a reference is made to the resurrection, you would have a collection of writings so mutilated that what remained could not be understood."

## What If Christ Be Not Risen?

If Christ be not risen all is vanity. That's the way Paul

described it. Five times he used the word "vain," which means "empty," "senseless," "worthless," "no good."

What is it Paul said was vain? You "believed in vain" (1 Corinthians 15:2). In other words, a Christian's belief is empty, senseless, worthless—unless Christ is risen from the dead according to the Scriptures. There isn't any other way into His kingdom.

Without the Resurrection God's grace is in vain. Is it possible for God's grace to be worthless? Yes, without the Resurrection it is vain, worthless, because God's plan for our redemption would have failed.

Furthermore, Paul declared that his preaching was vain—useless, no good, empty. Not only was his preaching vain without the risen Christ, but any preaching that leaves out the risen Christ is utterly useless and worthless.

## But Christ Is Risen!

Christ's resurrection, however, is a fact: "He rose again the third day according to the Scriptures" (1 Corinthians 15:4). Only John seemed to be convinced of the Resurrection by the empty tomb and grave clothes. These became further evidences to the other disciples, but only after Jesus had presented himself to them at various places and times. The empty tomb was a point of contention. The chief priests and elders accused the disciples of opening the tomb and stealing Christ's body. It became a matter of one testimony against the other, neither side having evidence to prove their case, except the testimony of perjured soldiers.

The clincher in the claim was Jesus himself. People could go on arguing about the tomb, but Jesus was alive, and He left more evidence than would be necessary in any court of law to prove the claim of His case.

Luke, a doctor by profession, was accustomed to making decisions based on facts. In his recording of the Acts of the Apostles he used some medical terminology. Speaking of Jesus he wrote, "He showed himself alive after his passion by many infallible proofs, being seen of them [i.e., the disciples] forty days, and speaking of the things pertaining to the kingdom of God" (Acts 1:3). In the original text, the term "infallible proofs" could be rendered "infallible symptoms"—more in keeping with Luke's approach. He undoubtedly meant to express the certainty of a conclusion based on proofs.

Peter's sermon to the Gentiles in the house of Cornelius was recorded by Luke. Peter said,

> Him God raised up the third day, and showed him openly; not to all the people, but unto witnesses chosen before of God, even to us, who did eat and drink with him after he rose from the dead (Acts 10:40,41).

## Eyewitnesses

Have you ever seen a criminal lawyer in the courtroom as he confronts a witness on the stand? As forcefully and dramatically as possible the lawyer reaches for the one question he hopes will win his case. He asks, "Did you actually see the defendant? Can you point him out? Is he in this room?" The judge, the jurors, and the attorneys accept the testimony of eyewitnesses as conclusive evidence.

The apostle Paul presented an unbreakable case for the resurrection of Jesus. He listed an amazing lineup of eyewitnesses. The evidence was so overwhelming that Paul probably had no intention of arguing a case for the truth of the Resurrection; he only mentions the eyewitnesses as a matter of record.

The first eyewitness Paul mentioned was Peter. "He

was seen of Cephas" (1 Corinthians 15:5). Various conjectures can be offered for Peter's being mentioned first. The blustery fisherman might have been the one who most needed the assurance that Christ was indeed alive—and forgiving.

In the same breath, Paul included the 12 disciples, "then of the twelve" (1 Corinthians 15:5). (This phrase is to be understood as more or less an official designation of Jesus' chosen following, not as an actual numbering—Judas had counted himself out.) These chosen witnesses whose spirits had been so depressed were revitalized by His appearance.

Lest there be anyone who might think the authenticity of the Resurrection was calculated upon alleged appearances to His close company of followers, Paul states, "He was seen of above five hundred brethren at once" (1 Corinthians 15:6). It seems Paul was saying to the doubter, "Check out my claim. Most of the 500 are still alive, although some have died. Ask them. Let them tell you whether or not they saw the risen Christ."

James is the next eyewitness. "He was seen of James" (1 Corinthians 15:7). It is believed that this was James, the brother of Jesus. He was at one time an unbeliever, but like Paul he was coverted to follow the Lord.

There is no way of knowing how many may have been included in " . . . then of all the apostles" (1 Corinthians 15:7). But it obviously was not restricted to the Twelve.

And finally, Paul said, "And last of all he was seen of me also, as of one born out of due time" (1 Corinthians 15:8). Paul didn't have the privilege of seeing Jesus as the others did. But his encounter was not any less convincing. He refers to his experience on the Damascus road when he was struck blind and then later healed at the hands of Ananias. He knew instantly that Christ was alive, for he had seen Him face to face.

Besides being seen by many at the same time, Jesus was also seen in a variety of places and at different times: in a garden, in a room, on a road, by a sea, on a mountain; at dawn, in the daytime, at night. Furthermore, Jesus stayed around long enough for His presence to be well documented. For 40 days He made appearances. During that time He ate with some of the witnesses, and He taught them. He didn't rush away; no one could say His presence was a mere apparition.

## The Trumpet Call

In an old Bible, more than 100 years old, are some paraphrased Scripture passages that were sung in the Church of Scotland. This is the way they sang 1 Thessalonians 4:13-18:

> Take comfort, Christians, when your friends in Jesus fall asleep; their better being never ends; why then dejected weep? Why inconsolable, as those to whom no hope is giv'n? Death is the messenger of peace, and calls the soul to heav'n. As Jesus dy'd, and rose again victorious from the dead; so His disciples rise and reign, with their triumphant Head. The time draws nigh, when from the clouds Christ shall with shouts descend, and the last trumpet's awful voice the heav'ns and earth shall rend. Then they who live shall changed be, and they who sleep shall wake; the graves shall yield their ancient charge, and earth's foundations shake. The saints of God, from death set free, with joy shall mount on high; the heav'nly host with praises loud shall meet them in the sky.

That's what Paul had preached and taught at Thessalonica just 5 years before coming to Corinth. Now some were saying in effect, "There is no resurrection, dead is dead!"

Paul set forth the proofs of Christ's resurrection very factually and logically. He had firmly established Christ's resurrection in order to relate it to the believer's resurrection. Paul placed in sequence the bodily resurrection of Christ and that of the Christian. If Christ was raised, the Christian will be raised; if Christ is dead—we are yet in our sins and most miserable.

## But . . .

A foreign diplomat had to listen to a government official give a speech in a language the diplomat could not understand. He told his interpreter to just paraphrase what was being said. Then he added, "However, if at any time he uses the word *but* I want to know every word that follows, just as he says it!" The word *but* can alter or even completely reverse everything that has been previously said.

The apostle Paul said: "But now is Christ risen from the dead, and become the firstfruits of them that slept" (1 Corinthians 15:20). He swept away all the arguments.

What a grand view Paul had of the redemption story. He reached back to the beginning of history: "For as in Adam all die, even so in Christ shall all be made alive. But every man in his own order: Christ the firstfruits" (1 Corinthians 15:22,23).

Then, after "Christ the firstfruits" of the resurrection, Paul looked down through the centuries, and spoke of those who are Christ's "at his coming." Just as there was the undeniable physical, bodily resurrection of Christ, there will be another resurrection day, a day when all who have surrendered their lives to Christ down through the ages will live again. "The graves shall yield their ancient charge, and earth's foundations shake."

# 5

## *All Men Are Sinners*

All have sinned, and come short of the glory of God (Romans 3:23).

I called at the home of a bereaved husband the day of his wife's funeral. They had been close companions; she would be sorely missed. I assured him that she had only put off the earthly dwelling place and someday there would be a reunion. He squeezed my hand as he said, "I want you to come back and talk to me about that."

Nearly a week passed before I could return. As I walked across the porch of the farmhouse, the lights were on and I saw him sitting in the chair beside a huge stack of Christian magazines, books, and periodicals. These were among the materials his dear, godly wife had regularly read. He was diligently searching through them.

He asked me to tell him more about my comments of a week ago. I began very simply to explain the way of salvation, carefully reading appropriate Scripture passages and explaining the applications. After making a complete presentation, I asked if he wanted to accept Jesus Christ into his life. His response surprised me. "Now don't you think God would think that was kind of foolish of me? After all, for many years I've served in various capacitites in the church. I've been a board member, Sunday school superintendent, Sunday school teacher, and served in other responsibilities. I've never done anything really bad. I've never cheated anyone. I don't use bad language. I don't smoke or drink."

He couldn't comprehend that he wasn't good enough. He could see that some people needed to have their lives changed, but he didn't. He could not understand that "all have sinned, and come short of the glory of God" (Romans 3:23).

## All Are Sinners

That's kind of hard to take for some folks, especially those who have not stooped to gross and unseemly conduct. They have treated their neighbors decently, living by standards of discipline that are rare among the majority in society.

Take a closer look at the third chapter of Romans. Verse 23 says, "All have sinned"; verse 9, "All under sin"; verse 12, "All gone out of the way"; verse 19, "All . . . guilty"; and in Romans 5:12, "All have sinned." So I guess that's exactly what was meant—"ALL."

Paul classified all of mankind into two groups: (1) heathen, or Gentiles, and (2) Jews.

## Ungodly Heathen

Paul didn't use the word *heathen*. But that's our understanding of the kind of people he described—the ungodly, the unrighteous—people who could excuse themselves on the grounds of ignorance, having not heard, or having no one to preach the gospel to them. Someone is always bringing up the heathen as a supposed argument against God's plan of redemption. Do such people deserve eternal punishment? Are the heathen really lost? How can they be expected to know and worship God?

The apostle Paul did not present a defense of his position, only a statement. He said they do deserve the wrath of God, "because that which may be known of God is manifest in them; for God hath showed it unto them. . . . So that they are without excuse: because that, when they knew God, they glorified him not as God" (Romans 1:19-21).

Why do they deserve God's wrath? Because they knew about Him and did not glorify Him.

## Gentile Moralizers

The "all" who have sinned included the Gentile moralizers who were prone to put on a front of being one thing while living another way. They were quick to judge others for their conduct, while they were doing the same thing themselves. Basically, the attitude of the Gentiles was this: Since we are not under Jewish law, we have freedom to live as we want. They flouted the goodness and mercy of God.

Why were they guilty? They knew the truth and did not obey it. That is the sin they were charged with—knowing and not dong, having light but not living in it.

## No Exceptions

If anyone ever had the advantage, it was the Jews. They were the possessors and keepers of the oracles of God, the divinely inspired writings of the prophets. In them they were instructed in worship and conduct. The Jews had been taught these from their youth. In fact, they prided themselves on keeping the Law. But the Law cannot save the Jew, circumcision cannot save the Jew, and birth cannot save the Jew.

The charge Paul pressed against the Jews was that they had not done any better at living in the light of their heritage than the Gentiles. And God is no respecter of persons. "As many as have sinned without law shall also perish without law; and as many as have sinned in the law shall be judged by the law" (Romans 2:12). Another paraphrasing of "no respecter of persons" is, "There is not a single exception."

## It Is Written

The pattern set by Jesus in His earthly ministry was carried on by Paul: Both referred to the Scriptures as authoritative. In the Epistle to the Romans, 19 times Paul repeated, "It is written." The Word of God is where you need to go to find out the truth; any other source will lead you astray. Philosophies, religions, and sciences offer explanations for man's condition. There have been, and still are, those who would like to convince us that "everyday in every way, man is getting better and better." Others blame "surroundings" for man's sinful condition. Still others rationalize behavior by attributing man's problem to the diseases of mankind.

Paul called the whole thing sin. "All have sinned, and come short of the glory of God" (Romans 3:23) conveys the meaning of the "guilt" of sin as well as the "power" of sin. In verse 9, "under sin" connotes the "bondage of sin."

In order to show man's depravity, Paul reached back into Genesis and on through the Law and the Prophets. His descriptions in Romans 3 were taken from the 14th and 53rd Psalms. Paul listed 14 charges that must be considered:

1. "There is none righteous, no, not one" (Romans 3:10).
2. "There is none that understandeth" (v. 11).
3. "There is none that seeketh after God" (v. 11).
4. "They are all gone out of the way" (v. 12).
5. "They are together become unprofitable" (v. 12).
6. "There is none that doeth good, no, not one" (v. 12).

7. "Their throat is an open sepulchre" (v. 13).
8. "With their tongues they have used deceit" (v. 13).
9. "The poison of asps is under their lips" (v. 13).
10. "Whose mouth is full of cursing and bitterness" (v. 14).
11. "Their feet are swift to shed blood" (v. 15).
12. "Destruction and misery are in their ways" (v. 16).
13 ."The way of peace have they not known" (v. 17).
14. "There is no fear of God before their eyes" (v. 18).

## Sinful Character

The first six of these charges reveal the *character* of a totally depraved man. By nature, no one is righteous. The depraved man does not understand *rightness* in his relationships. Not only does he not seek after God, but he goes out of his way in self-indulgence. The word "unprofitable" is an enlightening one. It means "turned sour," "good for nothing." It certainly is understandable that "no good" will come out of that kind of character.

## Sinful Speech

The *speech* of a totally depraved man is described in Romans 3:13,14. Jesus said, "Out of the abundance of the heart the mouth speaketh" (Matthew 12:34). Paul said the throat of a corrupted person is like the stench of a decaying body. The stench is in the words coming out of the person. To this is added the deceitfulness of the tongue. It has been said the tongue has the ability to charm like a melodious instrument or to cut like a murderous dagger. James said in his epistle, "The tongue is a fire, a world of iniquity. . . . The tongue can no man tame" (James 3:6,8). And, Paul continued, the lips are like a venomous snake, capable of deadly attacks.

## Sinful Conduct

A depraved man's *conduct* is further revelation of his sinful character. "Their feet are swift to shed blood" (Romans 3:15). It is not a pleasant picture, but it is one we see nearly every day. While I am writing these words a man is being strapped into an electric chair. He will be executed for the murder of four people—a mother and her three children. Among his last words were, "I'm not sorry. I have no remorse. It just happened."

Generation after generation of experience has proved that the life divorced from God is subject to rapid degeneration. The path leads downhill all the way. A twisted character will be characterized by blasphemy, murder, and destruction. "Destruction and misery are in their ways" (v. 16). "The way of peace have they not known" (v. 17). Untold misery emanates from a life void of peace. Constant turmoil churns within. The depraved man is a slave in his own prison.

## Turned Sour

There must be a cause for this soul having "turned sour." Paul's last indictment is the root of man's problem. It is stated so very clearly: "There is no fear of God before their eyes" (Romans 3:18). Solomon says in the Book of Proverbs that the fear of the Lord is the beginning of knowledge. David, the Psalmist, said: "The fear of the Lord is clean, enduring for ever" (Psalm 19:9). Another way that may be stated is "Reverence for the Lord is a pure and lasting way of life" (*The Psalms for Today*, R.K. Harrison). In another psalm he said: "Fear the Lord, . . . there is no want to them that fear him" (Psalm 34:9). What a contrast between those who fear the Lord and those who flout Him. Without fear or reverential trust in God, life has no checks and balances.

## One Thing God Can't Do

Only one thing God cannot do. He cannot save a man until that man sees himself as guilty and condemned. Jesus said, "They that be whole need not a physician, but they that are sick" (Matthew 9:12). If the world can save itself, it doesn't need a Saviour.

We have just read an awful description of mankind in God's Word. Man doesn't come out looking very good.

## A Blob of Nothing?

You can't read the Bible without realizing that man is lost. But does that mean he's a blob of nothing? Should he just throw up his arms and quit? He's in a pretty bad condition. But remember, man is made in the image of God. That must mean he's more than just human garbage, no matter how low he may have sunk.

Man is not just a cog in some big machine wound up by God. He really can be somebody and do something that will count for time and eternity. From the Biblical perspective, man is lost, but he is great. The gospel does not destroy the dignity of man. It does, in fact, give him purpose and meaning in life and in death.

## A New Creature

Any man touched by God could be another Paul, John, Elijah or Moses. For a life that is completely yielded to God the possibilities are limitless. What man can not do for himself, God can do for him.

The late Warren B. Stratton was an artist, sculptor, violin maker, and college professor. He loved his studio-workshop where he often restored ancient paintings or created his own. One day he picked up a rough, crude hunk of wood, and while looking as it admiringly, he said, "Isn't that a beautiful violin?" What he saw and what others saw were two different things. He saw the potential. He saw the final product after the hours of creative work.

God looks at man that way. He sees beyond the flaws and imperfections to what man can become.

## Real Dynamite

Paul was talking about this end product when he said: "I am not ashamed of the gospel of Christ: for it is the power of God unto salvation" (Romans 1:16). The word "power" is *dunamis* in the original text. That's the word we get *dynamite* from. Paul did not say the gospel contains power, or that it is powerful—He said the gospel is dynamite! It *is* power!

The message is that it takes a lot of power to change man. In fact, it takes more power than any mere man has. The power of the gospel can take a sinner who is totally depraved in body, soul, and spirit, and in a moment's time blast the sin right out of his life, making him a different person.

"If any man be in Christ, he is a new creature: old things are passed away; behold all things are become new" (2 Corinthians 5:17).

# 6
## *Salvation*

God commendeth his love toward us, in that, while we were yet sinners, Christ died for us (Romans 5:8).

At the age of 27, Martin Luther was sent to Rome on church business. He believed that good works done in Rome had more merit than those done in any other place.

Watching people climb on bare knees the staircase allegedly brought from Pilate's house in Jerusalem, Martin Luther set out to follow them in meritorious penance. As he crawled up the steps, he bent over and kissed each one. Suddenly an illuminating thought aroused his conscience, *The just shall live by faith.* He said it was as if God himself had spoken to him. He arose from his knees and rushed away from the place full of shame and remorse.

The Word of God came to him, Romans 1:17 in fact: "Therein is the righteousness of God revealed from faith to faith: as it is written, The just shall live by faith." There was no other source for his aroused conscience.

The Word of God reveals the value of a man as a person, giving meaning to life on earth and a hope for heaven above, through faith in our Lord Jesus Christ.

The problems of our world will never be resolved by all of the rationalistic and philosophical attempts that may be made. Salvation for mankind comes from God and He has made provision for man's salvation as revealed in the faith chapter of Romans.

## The Just Shall Live by Faith

*Justify or justification* is a legal term. To be justified is to be pardoned, acquitted. It means that sinners are made acceptable to God and regarded as righteous. But justification is done for us by God. No one can stand before a judge and pardon himself. This is the theme the apostle Paul emphasized throughout the Roman epistle. Seven times he used some form of the word *justification*.

The very fact that justification must be done for us means two things in particular: First, no amount of goodness, self-righteousness, or meritorious service warrants God's justification. Second, no matter how deep in sin a person has gone, it is possible for him to be pardoned on the merits of Jesus Christ.

## Faith, Not Feeling

Justification hinges on faith, not feeling. Some people place an undue emphasis on feeling good, including feeling good in your religious experience. But this idea of always feeling a certain way can be misleading. And when it comes to salvation, *knowing* is far more important than *feeling*—good or bad! Until you know from the Word of God that you are saved, feeling is irrelevant. Even after you know, feelings can be irrelevant: The enemy can make you feel guilty; even your own heart can condemn you (see 1 John 3:20). But "God is greater than our heart." Faith tells me to take God at His Word.

Salvation depends upon the Word and the person of Jesus Christ; "By grace are ye saved through faith" (Ephesians 2:8). Fruit and feeling follow. Never the other way around. Otherwise salvation *would* be "by works of

49

righteousness." After faith comes the most sought after fruit of righteousness in all the world—peace. "We have peace with God through our Lord Jesus Christ" (Romans 5:1).

## The Search Is Over

"We have peace." What an experience; what a feeling! The search is over; the prize is found. You don't have to go on, endlessly trying this and that to find peace. When I have had the privilege to be used of God in leading a soul to Christ, often one of the first involuntary expressions of the new convert has been a sigh, an expression of relief; peace is taking over. The running can stop now. All the defenses can be dropped. Peace with God means harmony with God. Life takes on new dimensions. Peace means freedom from fear, release from tension, assurance, confidence, tranquility.

A troubled conscience is a tyrant. It steals our sleep, puts rocks in our pillow, and blocks out the sunshine. Peace with God means peace with our own conscience. Peace with God also means peace despite the enemy of our souls. "Peace I leave with you, my peace I give unto you: not as the world giveth, give I unto you. Let not your heart be troubled, neither let it be afraid" (John 14:27). "And the peace of God, which passeth all understanding, shall keep your hearts and minds through Christ Jesus" (Philippians 4:7).

## Walk In, the Door's Open

In addition to peace, "we have access by faith into this grace wherein we stand" (Romans 5:2). In the ancient days of kings, a man could be killed for approaching a king. A person had to have an invitation and be presented to a king according to an elaborate protocol. Paul said that's all done away with: You don't have to go through anyone else; you don't need an invitation—the door is wide open. Walk in and talk to the King. That is the provision of salvation. Jesus made the way possible when He presented us faultless to the Father. "Through him we both have access by one Spirit unto the Father" (Ephesians 2:18).

## God's No Sad Sack

God didn't give us some long-faced sad salvation. We don't need to go through life afraid of fun and enjoyment. God's no sad sack. Take a look in your Bible and you will find 485 times some form of the words *joy, joyous,* or *rejoice.* In this fifth chapter of Romans, three times Paul describes the results of justification in terms of joy: "We . . . rejoice in hope." "We glory [rejoice] in tribulations." "We . . . joy [rejoice] in God" (Romans 5:2,3,11).

## Rejoice in Hope

"Hope" as used in this text means to anticipate with pleasure and great expectation. Hope is always projecting into the future. The unsaved often accuse the Christians of a pie-in-the-sky religion. In some ways they are right. We do have something to look forward to: Everything God has promised is going to come to pass. We do have something to rejoice about: "Now are we the sons of God, and it doth not yet appear what we shall be: but we know that, when he shall appear, we shall be like him; for we shall see him as he is" (1 John 3:2).

In his epistle to Titus, Paul wrote: "We should live soberly, righteously, and godly, in this present world; looking for that blessed hope, and the glorious appearing of the great God and our Saviour Jesus Christ" (Titus 2:12,13).

Call it pie-in-the-sky if you will. It is a blessed hope—so rejoice in it and be glad. You should have left your sadness on the other side, when you were among those "without Christ, . . . strangers from the covenants of promise, having no hope, and without God in the world" (Ephesians 2:12).

## Rejoice In Tribulation?

Trouble is usually considered antagonistic to joy. Sorrow and tears accompany trouble. But not of necessity. Paul spoke of himself "as sorrowful, yet alway rejoicing; as poor, yet making many rich; as having nothing, and yet possessing all things" (2 Corinthians 6:10). His example says we should rejoice in trouble. The unbeliever can't do that. This present life is all he has and he isn't too secure in it, so when trouble comes it is calamitous.

This is not so with those who by faith have accepted salvation through the Lord Jesus Christ. No matter how dark the way, the believer knows the morning will come.

Our joy is not confined to the future. We rejoice here and now, susceptible as life is to heartache and sorrow. We do not escape this world. We rejoice in spite of tribulations.

We are told to rejoice in troubles because they are fleeting—here today and gone tomorrow. We rejoice because when the Lord takes us through them, they make us a better person: "Our light affliction, which is but for a moment, worketh for us a far more exceeding and eternal weight of glory" (2 Corinthians 4:17).

Paul said in Romans 5:3 that "tribulation worketh patience." The word "patience" has associated with it a joyous disposition (see, for example Hebrews 10:34 and James 1:2). Tribulation teaches us not to grimly bear up but to joyfully bear up. God knows what we all need. When troubles come, our old Adamic nature wants to rebel and ask why, to grumble and complain. But God gives more grace at those moments, and when we come through the trial we have added more strength and patience to our character.

From "patience" we go to "experience." In the original text "experience" means the results of being proved, or tested. Other translations speak of "maturity of character." You have tribulation and it produces in you patience. Your patience is an experience of proving or maturing your character as a child of God.

Paul continued the sequence of reasons for rejoicing. He said that character development works hope, "hope of the glory of God" (Romans 5:2). "And hope maketh not ashamed" (Romans 5:5). He has come right back to the "blessed hope." One thing is added that is reassuring, you'll not be ashamed. In other words, you're not going to be disappointed. You're not going to regret that your life has been motivated by that hope.

## Rejoice in God

Most Jews regarded God with awe. He was a thundering voice from heaven, a pillar of cloud and fire, a sender of rain, or fire and brimstone. Then Jesus came, introducing God as the Heavenly Father. Consider, for example, the Parable of the Prodigal Son, perhaps better titled the Parable of the Loving Father. Jesus struck a note of rejoicing. Through Him man's relationship to God was changed. His atonement on the cross bridged the gap that was created back in the Garden.

Paul elaborates further upon the Atonement:

> By one man sin entered into the world, and death by sin; and so death passed upon all men, for that all have sinned. . . . For if by one man's offense death reigned by one; much more . . . the gift of righteousness shall reign in life by one, Jesus Christ (Romans 5:12,17).

So rejoice in God. He calls us to himself through Jesus

Christ. And Jesus introduces the Almighty Heavenly Father who loves us. Rejoice, you are loved by the Creator himself.

## Love So Amazing, So Divine

"God commendeth his love toward us, in that, while we were yet sinners, Christ died for us" (Romans 5:8). This is the heart of salvation—God so loved the world. The world has never seen such a display of love as was shown by God sending Jesus into our world. God was willing to send His own Son to be buffeted, scourged, and crucified by wicked men. What a sacrifice to make for our sakes when He gave His Son to die for us all.

We could never be sustained through life if it weren't for "the love of God . . . shed abroad in our hearts by the Holy Ghost" (Romans 5:5). What a confidence we have knowing that His love is in our hearts.

"Behold, what manner of love the Father hath bestowed upon us, that we should be called the sons of God" (1 John 3:1). God's love knows no limit. No sinner is too bad for Him to love; no breach too great for Him to bridge; no pain too deep for Him to solace.

The salvation of God is all out of proportion to our importance or worth. No wonder we find it so difficult to comprehend. "Hallelujah, what a thought! Jesus *full* salvation brought." His character is bound up in it. He means every word of every promise. He wants them to be claimed, against the day of our ultimate salvation.

> For I am persuaded, that neither death, nor life, nor angels, nor principalities, nor powers, nor things present, nor things to come, nor height, nor depth, nor any other creature, shall be able to separate us from the love of God, which is in Christ Jesus our Lord (Romans 8:38,39).

# 7

## *How To Be Saved*

> If thou shalt confess with thy mouth the Lord Jesus, and shalt believe in thine heart that God hath raised him from the dead, thou shalt be be saved (Romans 10:9).

"I'm cramming for the finals" was the reason given by a professor for quitting his 40-year teaching career to begin memorizing the Bible. He realized a time of accounting was coming, and the only way he saw to prepare for it was to memorize the Bible. It would be a big task to memorize 31,173 verses!

If the man did accomplish the feat, that in itself would not prepare him for the finals. In fact, he would be doing the very thing that Paul said was a "zeal of God, but not according to knowledge" (Romans 10:2).

He was right about one thing—the Bible is the place to find the answers. However, the answers are not in memorizing the Bible, but in obedience to it.

The apostle Paul was truly a godly man. His heart was moved with compassion for people. He prayed for them. He wanted them to be saved. This was the motivation that impelled Paul. In the first chapter of his epistle to the Romans, Paul wrote, "I am debtor both to the Greeks, and to the Barbarians; both to the wise, and to the un wise. I am ready to preach the gospel . . . for it is the power of God unto salvation" (Romans 1:14-16).

But he was especially concerned about his own people. He sought above everything "that they might be saved" (Romans 10:1).

Many people today are just like his people: good people, people full of zeal for God, people with high principles, people who work hard for the church. They have good intentions, and they want to be righteous—or right. But they are ignorant of what true righteousness is, and how it is to be obtained. They believe their good works will establish their own righteousness.

Paul described how all men are sinners, and how the whole world is guilty before God. He reviewed the whole plan of redemption by first telling the Jews how they could not be saved. You cannot be saved by zeal, or by establishing your own righteousness, or by the keeping of Moses' law.

All of our works, whether they are inside or outside the church, can never, never save us. In fact, the Bible calls our so-called good works "filthy rags" (Isaiah 64:6). Some people believe if they participate in all of the sacraments of the church they will be righteous. It just isn't so. Going to church, as good as that can be, won't save anyone.

These are the points Paul was explaining to the Jews. He told them he appreciated their zeal—but it was misdirected. They had righteousness—but it was self-righteousness and it would not be accepted by God.

## *Close* Counts only in Horseshoes

I'm sure you've heard it many times, as I have: "*Close* doesn't count except in horseshoes." That's about what Paul said, in Romans 10. The Amplified translation, verse 8, reads, "The Word (God's message in Christ) is near you, on your lips and in your heart; that is, the Word—the message, the basis and object—of faith, which we preach." So near—almost, but not in. The Word was in their minds and hearts but not believed.

The steps to salvation are simple. They are contained in a few small words. The first word is *faith*. So many people have stumbled over that little word. "I can't understand," they say. "It's walking blind. How do you expect me to do that?" But you live by faith every day in dozens of ways. You sit and watch a beautiful color television set. Do you understand how that picture, in living color, gets into your living room only seconds after the camera was turned on halfway around the world? You don't understand all the technological things that happen, but you accept the results. You know when you turn on the switch that the lights will come on. That's exactly the way it is with faith.

> The wind bloweth where it listeth, and thou hearest the sound thereof, but canst not tell whence it cometh, and whither it goeth: so is every one that is born of the Spirit (John 3:8).

Faith is laying hold of Christ, for He is the object of our faith. It is not simply a subjective feeling, but an objective act.

## Confess

The second step in being saved is *confess*. "Confess with thy mouth the Lord Jesus, . . . with the mouth confession is made unto salvation" (Romans 10:9,10).

*Confess* is not a very big word, but it's a great big step. This isn't *confession* in the sense of private acknowledgement of offense to a brother. This is public declaration that Jesus Christ is Lord. An inference drawn from silent discipleship will not do. *Confession* means a declared discipleship, letting others know of your faith. You may have an opinion about Jesus Christ, but that opinion must bring action—action that speaks out.

It is not enough to inwardly cherish the convictions of our hearts or to confess to ourselves. It is not enough to confess to our friends who agree with us, or to even confess to God. It must include readiness to confess in public, before friend, foe, or the indifferent.

In the United States it is culturally acceptable to be religious. But to confess Jesus Christ is something else. It is saying, "I accept Jesus Christ as the promised Son of God." It also says, "I have a new relationship with my Heavenly Father." John described it like this: "Whosoever shall confess that Jesus is the Son of God, God dwelleth in him, and he in God (1 John 4:15).

John also shows us another side of confession. "If we confess our sins, he is faithful and just to forgive us our sins, and to cleanse us from all unrighteousness" (1 John 1:9). Notice, cleansing is conditional; "*If* we confess. . . ." Confession isn't optional; to be saved one must confess Jesus Christ as Lord and confess his sins.

To confess Christ means salvation; to deny Christ means damnation.

> Whosoever therefore shall confess me before men, him will I confess also before my Father which is in heaven. But whosoever shall deny me before men, him will I also deny before my Father which is in heaven (Matthew 10:32,33).

### Believe

Step three is *believe*. Here is another of those big little words. Some say the words should be inverted. You must believe before you can confess. Others say confession is an act of believing. It's really not so important which comes first; they both must be part of the action toward salvation.

"If thou shalt confess with thy mouth the Lord Jesus, and shalt believe in thine heart that God hath raised him from the dead, thou shalt be saved. For with the heart man believeth unto righteousness" (Romans 10:9,10).

In the Book of Acts the Philippian jailer asked Paul, "What must I do to be saved?" The answer was simple: "Believe on the Lord Jesus Christ, and thou shalt be saved" (Acts 16:30,31). This is so simple that many people stumble over it. They want to *do* something. But all that is required is to believe on the Lord Jesus Christ, and that God raised Him from the dead. You are not asked to amend your life in some way. You don't have to rearrange the relationships in your home. You are not required to give up your business or business associates. You aren't even asked to give up some habit that may be offensive to God. It is not reformation that is offered— it is salvation, and there is a great difference between the two. The first is the result of works, the other is the result of faith—confessing, believing, and receiving.

In John's gospel he too said salvation was dependent upon believing. Notice the repetition of the word (placed in italics) in these verses:

> God so loved the world, that he gave his only begotten Son, that whosoever *believeth* in him should not perish, but have everlasting life" (John 3:16).
>
> He that *believeth* on him is not condemned: but he that believeth not is condemned already, because he hath not believed in the name of the only begotten Son of God" (John 3:18).
>
> He that *believeth* on the Son hath everlasting life: and he that believeth not the Son shall not see life; but the wrath of God abideth on him" (John 3:36).

There are two sides: "believeth" and "believeth not." On one side are those who are saved and have eternal life; on the other side are the lost on whom the wrath of God abides. There is no neutral ground. All of mankind is divided into two groups—believers and unbelievers.

The division has always been about Jesus. John said, "He came unto his own, and his own received him not. But as many as received him, to them gave he power to become the sons of God, even to them that *believe* on his name" (John 1:11). Here, believing is receiving.

The steps are easy, but they must be taken to be effective. The moment one truly by faith confesses Christ, and believing receives Him, everything changes. In that moment you are saved, regenerated, made righteous, made a child of God, and your name is written in the book of life.

### Yesterday, Today, Forever

Salvation is complete; it includes the past, present, and future. Sins of the past are cleansed by Christ's sacrifice; the penalty has been paid "for the remission of sins that are past" (Romans 3:25). We are also saved from the power of sin in the present, "for sin shall not have dominion" over us (Romans 6:14). And, thank God, one day we shall be ushered into His glory where no sin can enter.

### All Sinners Can Be Saints

No one is excluded from salvation. If all have sinned, all can be saved: "God so loved the world . . . , " not just a certain race of people who kept a set of rules, or those who attained some degree of goodness. Witness the words of John and Paul: "Whosoever believeth," "Everyone that believeth," "Unto all . . . that believe," "Whosoever shall call." It is obvious that salvation is available to everyone. Exclusion is made by the individual himself when he says no to God. We can either accept and believe, or reject and deny.

A man went into a chapel to pray. There he found workmen repairing the building. They had covered the pulpit and the altar to protect them from dust. For a few moments the man stood looking around. Then he reached into his pocket, pulled out his personal business card, walked over and laid it on the altar, and left. Back in the corner of the chapel a woman knelt, her tears pooling in the sawdust. Her soul cried out to God. The man was following a pattern of form; the woman was seeking forgiveness and peace with God.

## Beautiful Feet

To carry the good news, God chose mortal men rather than celestial angels (see 2 Corinthians 4:7). Jesus chose 12 apostles, and He sent out 70 also. There have been all kinds of puns poked at preachers. Some people feel preachers are unneccessary, and still others say there is no distinction between preachers and laymen.

Regardless, God uses preaching as a way to disseminate the gospel. In Romans 10:14,15 Paul pointed out that it is impossible for people to call upon someone they have not believed in, and it is impossible to believe in someone they haven't heard about—and how shall they hear without a preacher? "It pleased God by the foolishness of preaching to save them that believe" (1 Corinthians 1:21). Paul explained to Titus that God had "in due times manifested his word through preaching" (Titus 1:3). Jesus commissioned His followers to "Go . . . and *preach* the gospel to every creature (Mark 16:15).

We aren't accustomed to complimenting anyone by telling them that they have beautiful feet. But that is what Paul said about those who preach the gospel. This was a figure of speech, perhaps reflecting originally the body language of a runner when he was carrying *good* news. Paul applies the phrase to the messenger of the gospel.

The gospel of peace and glad tidings of good things have been distorted by preachers who stand behind pulpits in churches across the nation, so how do you determine what is gospel and what isn't gospel? Here is the measuring stick: "Preach the word" (2 Timothy 4:2); "We preach not ourselves, but Christ Jesus the Lord" (2 Corinthians 4:5); "We preach Christ crucified" (1 Corinthians 1:23); "He preached unto them Jesus, and the resurrection" (Acts 17:18). After all, preaching is only a method of communicating. The presentation stands or falls on its content: the Word, the gospel, the foolishness of the cross!

## How Can I Get Faith?

It may be easy to understand "confess" and "believe," but what about "faith"? Where does this intangible element so necessary to salvation come from? Faith comes from hearing. Hearing what? The Word of God. If you want faith you listen for it. But don't listen to just anything or anyone.

Paul said if you want faith—faith comes from hearing the Word. Listen to the Word and accept it, then the seed of faith will begin to grow. Find a church where you hear the gospel being preached. Listen to those who preach Jesus Christ crucified and raised from the dead. Then do the work of God: "Believe on Him whom he hath sent" (John 6:29).

# 8

## *How To Live Victoriously*

> In all these things we are more than conquerors through him that loved us (Romans 8:37).

The traditionally celebrated birth of the Olympic games is 776 B.C. Thereafter the games were staged at 4-year intervals. Few enterprises created by man have lasted so long or been so influential. Their importance is indicated by the fact that time was measured in Olympiads, or 4-year cycles. The athletic participants were originally Greek men, but later others were admitted from surrounding colonies.

Before the competition all contestants, including their families and trainers, and judges swore a solemn oath to clean and fair competition and judging. Winners became national heroes. Their feats and skills were memorialized by poets, artists, and sculptors.

Perhaps the apostle Paul would not feel altogether out of place at the Superdome watching the Eagles and Raiders square off in a championship game. It seems very likely from the analogies Paul used that he was somewhat of a sports fan. Perhaps he attended the Olympics on his way through Athens. In Corinth Paul may have attended the competition of the Isthmian games. We do know that he was very familiar with the games, training, and conditioning necessary to win. Out of these concepts Paul introduced some basic principles of Christian life and conduct, principles that would one day lead to winning a far greater prize than the wilting laurels awarded at the stadiums.

## Life Is a Conflict

Using the reference of athletic contests, Paul spoke of life as a conflict. He likened the Christian life to a race. The Berkeley version of "they which run in a race" (1 Corinthians 9:24) is "those racing in the stadium." Life is also like a fight in which the fighter strives to win, not just beat the air. In Paul's epistle to the Ephesians the analogy of a wrestling match is used. In an even more serious view of the believers' walk, Paul said it was like warfare. "This charge I commit unto thee . . . that thou . . . mightest war a good warfare" (1 Timothy 1:18).

If anyone ever told you that once you became a Christian your pathway would be strewn with rose petals and that every day would be like heaven itself, they did not tell you the truth.

Although our redemption in Christ is free and complete, we will be continually contested by the enemy until the race is finished. Satan doesn't want you to live a victorious life. The more of God's blessings you appropriate for your life, the more hostile the devil becomes.

You are on the road to victory when you realize that life is a race, a prize fight, a wrestling match, a warfare! The sooner we realize these are the facts, the better off we will be. "For Satan must not be allowed to get the better of us; we know his wiles all too well" (2 Corinthians 2:11, *New English Bible*). One of those "wiles," or "devices," is that he is the "accuser of our brethren" (Revelation 12:10). He wages an unrelenting warfare of seducing men and women to neglect Bible study, prayer, witnessing, and fellowshipping with believers in a local assembly.

## Learn the Rules

The Olympic and Isthmian games had been conducted for many years even in Paul's day. They followed closely defined rules, rules of entrance into the games, rules of how each sporting event would function. Contestants and trainers studied the rules because they would be judged according to them.

Paul knew about this, declaring in his analogy: "I therefore so run, not as uncertainly" (1 Corinthians 9:26). In writing to young Timothy, Paul stated it more directly, telling him you can't win unless you compete "according to the rules." "If a man also strive for masteries, yet is he not crowned, except he strive lawfully" (2 Timothy 2:5).

If we are to live victoriously, our lives must be conducted according to The Book, God's Word. The Bible, given by God, is your textbook for life. Revealing Jesus Christ as the Saviour of man, the true and living way (see John 14:6), this book holds the only true pattern for living, the only authoritative rule for faith and practice.

## Read the Word

We must know what the Bible says. If we are to know it we must read it, regularly and systematically. The athletic competitor could never learn the rules of the game by indiscriminately opening the rule book to read wherever it happened to fall open.

"Till I come, give attendance to reading" (1 Timothy 4:13). That's what the Bible tells us to do. It takes time to read the Word, more time than many of us are willing to give. No wonder we do not know which way to turn when life becomes disrupted.

Even Jesus needed the Word. When He was being tempted of the devil, Jesus said, "It is written, That man shall not live by bread alone, but by every word of God" (Luke 4:4).

One of the natural results of living the Christian life is that at some time, somewhere, someone will ask a reason for your faith. Why do you live as you do? Why do you act and talk the way you do? Why don't you do some things other people do? "Be ready always to give an answer to every man that asketh you a reason" (1 Peter 3:15).

## Study the Word

Only one way will you be prepared to give a reason: by *study* of the Word. "Study to show thyself approved unto God, a workman that needeth not to be ashamed, rightly dividing the word of truth" (2 Timothy 2:15).

That doesn't mean all Christians have to go to Bible college or take a Bible correspondence course. We can study the Word by diligently applying ourselves to the Word in our devotions each day. Our reading of the Word can become a study if we do not hurriedly read it.

Study the Word to see what God is saying to you. Some people study the Bible to find some remote, unrelated Scripture that will reinforce what they already believe.

## Hide It in Your Mind

You not only need to read and study the Word; you need to memorize it. That is the only way you can really keep the Word. No one can take it away from you when you have it tucked away in your mind.

There is no greater prescription for living a life of victory than that demonstrated by the Psalmist:

*Thy word* have I *hid in mine heart*, that I might not sin against thee. Blessed art thou, O Lord: teach me thy statutes. I will meditate in thy precepts, and have respect unto thy ways. I will delight myself in thy statutes: *I will not forget thy word* (Psalm 119:11,12,15,16, italics mine).

I had one of those old-fashioned Sunday school teachers who believed young boys ought to memorize from the Scriptures. She did everything possible to motivate memorization. Many of those verses I learned as a boy later gave me purpose and direction as I matured.

Times may come when neither a Bible nor a scripturally well-read friend is near for divine solice. Hubert Schmidt, while languishing in a dank, dark prison cell, said, "The Word I had committed to my mind was the only thing that kept me a sane man."

## Self-Discipline

Another principle lifted from the athletic events for living a victorious life was discipline. "Every man that striveth for the mastery is temperate in all things. . . . But I keep under my body, and bring it into subjection" (1 Corinthians 9:25,27). Others translate the Greek word for "temperate" in the King James Version "self-control," "strict training," and *"restricts* himself." And the phrase *keep under my body* is translated "I beat my body," "buffet my body," and "handle it roughly."

Every great athlete would readily understand Paul's words. You can hear them in any athletic training room. Such are the words of hard disciplinary coaches who condition athletes to be winners.

Many rookie athletes have washed out of training camp because they were not physically fit. They could pass the doctor's examination, but their bodies weren't in shape. They were flabby and weak; soft from self-indulgent living.

Those who wanted to enter the Isthmian or Olympic games engaged in 10 months of rigorous conditioning, and certified their faithfulness in training. They had to be morally clean. They were led through the stadium for all to see, and if anyone could verify a contestant's guilt for a crime or depravity of life, he was disqualified.

When Paul said "I buffet my body," he was right in his analogy. Physical training is exactly that. It is excruciating and painful. Training means hours of exercise, running, weight lifting, and muscle tension.

Building muscles demands arduous exercises. Not only are the muscles increased and toned, but the lungs are expanded to accommodate the demands expected of them in contest. For athletes know that to be contenders they must be physically ready to compete.

To maintain such physical conditioning means constant self-discipline. It is a life-style of daily limitation. A lazy athlete will never successfully compete. Neither will a lazy Christian. Victorious living requires a life of discipline. This must be the course we take each day.

The Christian must control the desires of the body. The Bible calls it the desires of the flesh. The natural man reasons that the appetites, drives, and forces in his body were put there by God, so He must have meant for them to be gratified. But the Bible says that "if ye live after the flesh, ye shall die: but if ye through the Spirit do mortify [make to die] the deeds of the body, ye shall live" (Romans 8:13).

Not many people like to hear the words *discipline, self-denial,* or even *moderation.* But the concept behind these words is another key to victorious living. Our biggest difficulty is keeping physically fit, that is, keeping our body completely and absolutely under control.

A popular philosophy of life says "Do your own thing," "I've got to be me." The Bible says the opposite: "For me to live is Christ"; "He must increase, I must decrease"; I . . . bring it [i.e., the body] into subjection." Paul addressed young Timothy using the analogy between life and warfare:

> Endure hardness, as a good soldier of Jesus Christ. No man that warreth entangleth himself with the affairs of this life; that he may please him who hath chosen him to be a soldier (2 Timothy 2:3-4).

If you asked some people how to live a victorious life, they would probably have a lot to say about prayer, worship, and the operations of the gifts of the Spirit. These are important facets of Christian living, but victorious living is a manifestation of the fruit of the Spirit, especially temperance, more commonly known as self-control, keeping bodily lusts under control.

> Walk in the Spirit, and ye shall not fulfil the lust of the flesh. Now the works of the flesh are manifest, which are these, adultery, fornication, uncleanness, lasciviousness, idolatry, witchcraft, hatred, variance, emulations, wrath, strife, seditions, heresies, envyings, murders, drunkenness, revelings, and such like: . . . they which do such things shall not inherit the kingdom of God (Galatians 5:16,19-21).

### A Crown That Won't Tarnish

It's easy to imagine Paul sitting in the stadium watching the games. Winners were paraded around the stands as people cheered. The winners walked to the winner's circle where a garland of leaves was placed on their heads.

The crown is the symbol of reward. The apostle Paul said to Timothy,

> I have fought a good fight, I have finished my course, I have kept the faith: henceforth there is laid up for me a

crown of righteousness, which the Lord, the righteous judge, shall give me at that day: and not to me only, but unto all them also that love his appearing (2 Timothy 4:7,8).

The gift of righteousness is ours by faith. The crown of righteousness is the reward given to those who have run the race, who have fought the fight, who have been good soldiers, who have lived victoriously through Jesus Christ.

### Not a Castaway

The apostle Paul was not thinking about losing his salvation when he said, "Lest . . . I myself should be a castaway." He was speaking of a reward for service. He was saying, in effect, "I want to serve in such a way that I will have the Lord's approval when I stand before Him." Let us run the race determined to let nothing hinder us.

Lay aside every weight, and the sin which doth so easily beset us, and let us run with patience the race that is set before us, looking unto Jesus the author and finisher of our faith; who for the joy that was set before him endured the cross, despising the shame, and is set down at the right hand of the throne of God (Hebrews 12:1,2).

# 9

## *Walking in the Spirit*

If we live in the Spirit, let us also walk in the Spirit (Galatians 5:25).

What if someone told you there was a way to tranquilize the troubled mind, relieve insomnia-inducing anxiety, and help cure nervous disorders—all without drugs or medicine? Many people who have begun a walking program report these results. Walking will strengthen your heart and lungs. Walking has been a key to warding off lower back problems and improving posture and circulation. It also helps to lower the levels of cholesterol, and is an effective way of losing weight. These are just some of the claims that have been validated by doctors and physical fitness experts who claim that walking is the best all-around exercise.

### Walk in the Spirit

Now let us consider the benefits to the soul from "walking in the Spirit." This is the discipline Paul describes in chapter 5 of Galatians. The word *walking* as applied to the Christian's life is not the same as the physical walking exercise. "Walk," as used in Paul's message to the Galatians, is a figurative expression for one's conduct of life.

Jesus knew we would all need to walk in the Spirit.

He had seen what *self*-determination could do. Peter was a good example of that. Under hostile pressure, Peter denied even knowing about Jesus.

## The Comforter Needed

As His betrayal and crucifixion drew near, Jesus began preparing His disciples for the change in their relationship with Him. He would be gone. They would be left behind in a hostile world. "Ye are not of the world, . . . therefore the world hateth you" (John 15:19).

The disciples had been called and had faithfully followed Jesus. But events prior to His crucifixion were accompanied by new anxiety and confusion. The disciples understood what Jesus had told them, that is, they recognized the words, but they did not comprehend them. Jesus had begun by telling them, "Let not your heart be troubled. . . . I go to prepare a place for you" (John 14:1,2).

> And I will pray the Father, and he shall give you another Comforter, that he may abide with you for ever (John 14:16). . . . Nevertheless I tell you the truth; It is expedient for you that I go away: for if I go not away, the Comforter will not come unto you; but if I depart, I will send him unto you (John 16:7).

The rest is history. Jesus did go away. The apostles stood and watched Him go, looking "steadfastly toward heaven as he went up" (Acts 1:10). From there the apostles went to an upper room where they prayed until the Holy Ghost descended upon them and they began to speak with other tongues.

Today it doesn't make much difference what people say about that phenomenal experience. Millions of people all around the world, from every conceivable walk of life, rejoice in having received the infilling of the Holy

Spirit; and they speak in other tongues just as believers did on the Day of Pentecost.

However, the Holy Spirit wasn't sent just to make people speak in tongues. He was sent to be, as Jesus called Him, the Paraclete, variously translated "Comforter," "Helper," "Counselor," "Advocate," literally "one called alongside to help."

Until the Day of Pentecost, the disciples had relied on Jesus for everything. Now He was gone and they would need to learn to rely upon the Holy Spirit, for He would be with them as Jesus had been. No matter where they might go, the Holy Spirit would always be there.

Seemingly each body of believers needs to recognize and practice the Spirit's presence, just as the apostles did. The apostle Paul was concerned about the church in Galatia. The works of the flesh were too prevalent among them. Their spiritual natures were being overpowered by yielding to sinful gratifications. The apostle Paul knew there was only one way that the church in Galatia would ever be able to live above the lusts and desires of carnal appetites.

The formula was very simple, but effective. If you do not want to fulfill the lusts of the flesh, Paul said "you must live in the Spirit." Although such an injunction may sound a little superspiritual, Paul was careful to make it very practical.

To *walk* in the Spirit is not to *work* in the Spirit: "not of works, lest any man should boast" (Ephesians 2:9). Man's best efforts have failed too many times.

Walking in the Spirit doesn't imply that we sit in a darkened room in meditation, or that we wear sneakers and act strange. It doesn't even mean that we go around all day long mumbling prayers or audibly praising the Lord.

Walking in the Spirit means to live under a new control, to trust the Holy Spirit to do in you what you cannot do for yourself. Life takes on a completely different form than when you followed your natural desires.

## The Spirit Will Guide

God intended for His children to be spiritually healthy.

> Beloved, I wish above all things that thou mayest prosper and be in health, even as thy soul prospereth. For I rejoiced greatly, when the brethren came and testified of the truth that is in thee, even as thou walkest in the truth. I have no greater joy than to hear that my children walk in truth (3 John 2-4).

Jesus said the Holy Spirit is the Spirit of truth, and a guide into all truth. We wouldn't need a guide if right and wrong were always distinct.

How does right and wrong get confused? The "father of lies" is very subtle. As you look at the stark list of the works of the flesh in Galatians 5:19-21, you realize how in our day the devil has tried to dress them up to look acceptable. He likes it when people declare sin as sickness. We have been told over and over again that some abnormal life-styles are only alternative life-styles. With constant repetition, such lies may wear us down, weakening our will to resist them.

For our orientation to truth, we can take a lesson from flying: Instrument flying is relying on that panel of gauges and meters before us; seat-of-the-pants flying is relying on our instinct gained through experience. Flying without mechanical aid is okay for some circumstances, but when darkness, fog, or turbulence sets in, let's forget our instincts—how it feels, what everybody's doing—and go for the instruments—the Word of God, the guidance of His Spirit, the counsel of His people. Otherwise, we may choose the way that "seemeth right," but ends in death.

## The Spirit Will Teach

Jesus told His disciples, "The Holy Spirit . . . will teach you all things" (John 14:26, NIV). Jesus had been their teacher, but He was going away. The Holy Spirit would be the teacher that would continue to teach them. This school of the Spirit does not mean that we will be taught new truths. If that were the case we would have people trying to write a new Bible. What we may not learn from sermons, Bible lessons, or books, we learn from the Spirit who comes to open our eyes to the truth in the Word.

The Spirit doesn't teach us so we can be smarter than anyone else. He teaches us what we need to know so we can resist the works of the flesh that seek to entangle our lives. For it is only when our lives are consistent with our testimonies that they can be a positive influence in the world.

It is interesting to note that the Spirit's teaching includes jogging the memory. "He shall teach you all things, and bring all things to your remembrance, whatsoever I have said unto you" (John 14:26). We are so prone to forget. Jesus reproved the disciples: "Why do you reason among yourselves because you have brought no bread? Do you not yet understand, or remember the five loaves of the five thousand. . . . Nor the seven loaves of the four thousand and how many large baskets you took up" (Matthew 16:8-10, NKJV).

It would be impossible to number the many times that in a given situation—conversation, witnessing, preaching, or teaching—the Spirit has brought to my remembrance words of Scripture that were needed at that moment.

75

## The Spirit Reproves

Another ministry of the Spirit is to reprove the world of sin. The word *reprove* might better and more correctly be translated "convince." If you have ever attempted to lead a soul to Christ, you understand this unique ministry of the Spirit. No matter what you may say, no matter how logically you may have presented the gospel, unless the Spirit convinces men of the truth they will continue in their sin. Jesus said the Spirit "will reprove the world of sin, and of righteousness" (John 16:8). The Holy Spirit can cut through the wall of resistance that people build around themselves. He can melt hearts that have become hardened and stubborn. He can break through the haze of misunderstanding to convince men of their sin.

The Holy Spirit is not limited in how He convinces men of sin. He may use one of man's senses, such as the conscience, or He may use the Word that has been heard at one time or another. The Holy Spirit could even use a dream or a vision. But most often He uses a human instrument—people like you and me.

One of my most humbling and sobering experiences was to read a letter from a teenage girl. She said, "I have never met you, but I have heard you many times on your weekly radio broadcast. Yesterday you were in the town where I live. I was on my way home from school when I saw you and your wife get out of your car and walk down the sidewalk. I knew who you were from pictures I had seen. Just seeing you made me realize I was not right with God. I rushed home, went to my room, and asked God to forgive me of my sins." Today she is the wife of a pastor.

The Spirit does the convincing and convicting; we do our part by walking in the Spirit so He can shine through us.

The world can't comprehend the fact that Christ has already won the struggle between evil and righteousness. That's why it is easy for many people to believe that God is dead and that the Church is dying. Only as the Holy Spirit opens men's eyes do they realize that the devil is the "dead" one—he has been judged—and in God's time he will be put away forever. I can't convince men of that, and neither can you, but the Spirit can. In a moment He can reveal and heal a man's spiritual blindness, just as He did with Saul of Tarsus.

### The Spirit Reveals Christ

To walk in the Spirit is to move closer to the Lord Jesus Christ. For the Spirit does not bring new teaching of himself. Jesus said, "He shall glorify me" (John 16:14). To "glorify" Jesus means that the Holy Spirit makes Christ known in His full majesty.

In his book *The Normal Christian Life,* Watchman Nee tells about staying in the home of some friends on one of his trips to America. The couple urged him to pray for them. They were distressed because of family conflicts, irritations caused by their children, and losing their tempers. They asked him to pray for God to give them patience. When Mr. Nee replied, "That is one thing I cannot do," they were shocked. "God is not going to answer your prayer. Have you prayed that way; did God answer? Do you know why God did not answer? You don't need patience." With that the wife's eyes flashed and she burst out with, "What are you saying? We get irritated all day long. It doesn't make sense." Mr. Nee quietly replied, "It is not patience you have need of; it is Jesus."

The ministry of the Holy Spirit is to reveal, to guide, to illuminate. Just as the sun drives out the darkness, brightening the day, bringing light and life to all of creation; so does the Spirit to the heart of man. He reveals Jesus.

## The Spirit Helpeth Our Infirmities

Have you ever prayed, and prayed, and prayed, and it seemed your prayers never reached beyond the room you were in? Or have you ever been so deeply hurt or overwhelmed with grief that you couldn't find the words to pray? Paul had an experience like that. He had what he called "a thorn in the flesh." Three times he prayed for its removal, but no answer.

The Spirit brings a new dimension to praying.

> The Spirit also helpeth our infirmities: for we know not what we should pray for as we ought: but the Spirit itself maketh intercession for us with groanings which cannot be uttered (Romans 8:26).

We may be stymied. We may see no answers; we may see too many. The Spirit, however, is not perplexed. He takes the heart of the problem to the heart of the Father in a prayer of intercession. That means the Spirit "pleads" for the needs you don't even know how to pray for. What an adventure it is to walk in the Spirit!

## Keep in Step

Have you ever noticed how people walk? Some slouch along with drooping shoulders, dragging their feet in uncertain steps. Others walk with quick, short steps; still others seem to gallop along.

Paul was aware of the different ways people walk. In Galatians 5:16, when he said "walk in the Spirit," he used the word for "walk" that was used most commonly when referring to the physical movement of a body.

A few verses later he repeats his injunction: "If we

live in the Spirit, let us also walk in the Spirit" (Galatians 5:25). This time, however, he used a different word for walk. This word carried the connotation of walking in cadence, shoulders erect, chin up, and stepping out with a purpose. It means to keep in step with the Spirit, to walk with Him.

God doesn't want us just to saunter along, or to slouch through life. He wants us to walk in the Spirit, and to walk in confidence. As you do, the Holy Spirit will guide, teach, correct, reveal Jesus, and intercede for you. You cannot lose walking in the Spirit.

> If we live by the (Holy) Spirit, let us also walk by the Spirit.—If by the (Holy) Spirit we have our life [in God], let us go forward walking in line, our conduct controlled by the Spirit (Galatians 5:25, *Amplified Bible*).

# 10

## *To Show the Lord's Death (Communion and Baptism)*

> Reckon . . . yourselves to be dead indeed unto sin, but alive unto God through Jesus Christ our Lord (Romans 6:11).

My wife has a little seashell that was given to her by her mother. It was a memento she brought home from the World's Fair in Chicago. It wasn't of any great monetary value, just a keepsake with her name etched on the surface. As the years passed the seashell was pushed aside, eventually ending up in a box tucked away in the attic.

Shortly after her mother's death my wife ran across the seashell while looking for something else. It triggered a kaleidoscope of memories. The memories were warm and pleasant, of love, thoughtfulness, and care.

The same kind of thoughts come to my mind when I walk past our guest bedroom and see my mother's old Singer sewing machine sitting under the windows. It's a keepsake she wanted me to have.

There are two symbolic ordinances observed by the Church: the believer's baptism and the Lord's Supper. Man has twisted and grossly misrepresented both of them to one degree or another—shrouding them in mysticism on the one hand, reducing them to insignificant symbolism on the other. Endless controversies have swirled around them, volumes being written to support the various viewpoints.

## Hocus-Pocus?

There is a story offered by an English clergyman of the 17th century that the word *hocus-pocus,* which we use to mean "trickery or deception," is a corruption of some of the Latin words used in the Catholic Mass. Objecting to the idea of transubstantiation, the bread and wine actually becoming the body and blood of Christ, critics of the Catholic church supposedly felt a bag of tricks was being foisted upon worshipers: *Hoc est corpus* ("This is the body") being only so much *hocus-pocus.*

And today Christianity has critics who feel the same way, looking upon the ordinances of Communion and water baptism as superstitious escapes from reality. They claim these ordinances are crude, primitive, and unholy.

## Where Did the Ordinances Come From?

What about these ordinances? Are they vain traditions of church life? Where did they come from?

The Bible says Jesus instituted both of them. At the feast of the Passover with His disciples Jesus instituted the Lord's Supper. It was by no means an elaborate ceremony, comprising no more than the breaking and eating of ordinary bread and the drinking of equally ordinary wine. These two simple acts were to be done "in remembrance" of Jesus (1 Corinthians 11:24).

Before Jesus left the earth He conducted a commissioning service with His disciples in which He said, "Go ye therefore, and teach all nations, *baptizing* them in the name of the Father, and of the Son, and of the Holy Ghost" (Matthew 28:19, italics added).

These two ordinances were to continue in the church, to be practiced by His believers "until He comes."

Men have gone to extremes in their interpretations of

81

these ordinances, and have often been careless in the observance of them.

There is indication that the Early Church practiced commemorating the Lord's Supper regularly. It appears to have been, at first, a daily custom among them. Later they met to keep it once a week. It was meant to be a continuing practice; however, no emphasis was placed upon the frequency of its observance.

It's a sad commentary upon human nature that man has abused everything God has given him. The church in Corinth had allowed the Lord's Supper to become profane. They were more taken up with eating and drinking to excess than in remembering Jesus. The *Lord's* Supper became *their* supper. The Lord was left out of it, and Paul told them they should stay at home to eat and drink, and not come to the church under the guise of remembering the Lord.

A lot of different activities go on in the church today. We don't have the practice of meeting for a meal to observe the Lord's Supper, so the abuse found in the church at Corinth does not enter into our observance today. However, it does remind us that we must not allow anything to profane our observance of the Lord's Supper.

In the church of Corinth the abuse was excess, perhaps ours is neglect; theirs was familiarity, perhaps ours is formality.

The tradition of the Lord's Supper is so strong that men and women of all persuasions, within and without the church, know the essential elements in its commemoration. It has been incorporated into the wedding ceremonies of both Catholics and Protestants as part of a ceremonial endorsement of blessing. Unfortunately within the church many accept it only as a form, part of their church ritual. They are blind to any spiritual and personal significance. It means no more to them than a good omen.

## The Same Night

The occasion of the Lord's Supper was not carelessly selected: It was "the same night in which he was betrayed" (1 Corinthians 11:23). A certain expectancy must have been among the disciples. The arrangements were already appointed. Jesus had instructed them:

> When ye are entered into the city, there shall a man meet you, bearing a pitcher of water; follow him into the house where he entereth in. And ye shall say unto the goodman of the house, The Master saith unto thee, Where is the guest chamber, where I shall eat the passover with my disciples? And he shall show you a large upper room furnished: there make ready. And they went, and found as he had said (Luke 22:10-13).

Jesus had found love and devotion in the fellowship of His followers. Now that they were about to part, Jesus made a permanent appointment with them so that until He returned they could have fellowship together about His table.

## It's Not in the Name

This blessed ordinance has been given several designations by men, none of them offensive; in fact, each was meant to enhance the occasion. For many years in Early Church history it was the Holy Eucharist, a joyous thanksgiving. To others it has been a sacrament, that is, an outward sign of an inward grace. It is also a Holy Communion. The apostle Paul referred to it as a communion in 1 Corinthians 10:16. It was meant to be a communion between the Lord and His believers. To many people, the most meaningful designation is the Lord's Supper, as recorded in 1 Corinthians 11:20.

## It's in His Name

The service was simple.

83

> The Lord Jesus . . . took bread: and when he had given thanks, he brake it, and said, Take, eat; this is my body, which is broken for you: this do in remembrance of me. After the same manner also he took the cup, when he had supped, saying, This cup is the new testament in my blood: this do ye, as oft as ye drink it, in remembrance of me. For as often as ye eat this bread, and drink this cup, ye do show the Lord's death till he come (1 Corinthians 11:23-26).

Nothing was said about posture, whether one needs to be standing, kneeling, sitting, or lying down. The only posture that needs to be considered is that of the heart and mind. Nor was there any mention of the place of observing the Lord's Supper, or of the use of certain furniture.

The Lord's Supper has been called a feast of remembrance.

The entire emphasis was and must continue to be that prescribed by Jesus: "In remembrance of me." Jesus must be the center of attention, especially His work on the Cross. No other focus is adequate to take us through life.

Prone to forget, man needs to be reminded. God commanded memorials on different occasions in the Old Testament. The Crucifixion and Resurrection (along with the Incarnation) are the most significant events in history. Jesus instituted a memorial surrounding them. He will remember us; let us not forget Him.

## A Divine Meal

Jesus knew only too well that there would be times when the only thing that would give encouragement would be to remember what He did for us. At times we are ready to quit. We have faced more sorrow, tragedy, and heartache than a lifetime can stand. We are helpless; we feel abandoned and forsaken.

The therapy for such experiences is not to give up hoping or to tune out the conflict. No amount of counseling or positive thinking will drive away the darkness. The appropriate response is to come to His table and hear once again, "This is my body broken for you . . . this is my blood shed for you . . . take, eat, drink, in remembrance of me." He gives peace. His presence drives away the darkness and gloom. That is the blessed fellowship of communion at the Lord's Supper: just to remember once again that the victory is not in struggling, not in anything else we can do, but in the finished work of Calvary.

We need the assurance of knowing that He has already embraced our loneliness and heartache. He struggled before we did and paid the supreme price for *all* our souls' needs.

## Self-Examination

Discipleship is based on love and obedience. At the last Passover Feast Jesus said, "If ye love me, keep my commandments. . . . If a man love me, he will keep my words. . . . He that loveth me not keepeth not my sayings" (John 14:15,23,24). The only prerequisite for participation in the Lord's Supper is discipleship. The command is imperative, "This do in remembrance of me."

But the Corinthians were including those who were not following the Lord in discipleship. Their keeping of the Lord's Supper had become a despicable sham. To correct the practice, Paul showed the Corinthians just how dangerous it was to profane the Lord's Supper.

Taking communion is serious business. Paul uses strong words to describe just how serious it is: "Whoever eats . . . or drinks . . . in an *unworthy* manner"—"without proper reverence" (Phillips), "in a way that dishonors him [i.e., Jesus]" (Today's English Version)—"will be guilty of the body and the blood of the Lord. . . . He . . . eats and drinks judgment to himself, not discerning the Lord's body. For this reason many are weak and sick . . . and many sleep [are dead]" (1 Corinthians 11:27,29,30, NKJV).

Now, examine yourself, and then eat at the Lord's Supper. To each individual is given the privilege and responsibility of taking a personal inventory.

> If we were closely to examine ourselves beforehand, we should avoid the judgment of God. But when God does judge us, he disciplines us as his own sons, that we may not be involved in the general condemnation of the world (1 Corinthians 11:31,32, Phillips).

## Repent and Be Baptized

The students at Louisiana Tech University had never seen anything happen at their campus like the baptismal service in the campus swimming pool. The group that was baptized represented an interesting cross section of students, including some outstanding athletes and popular coeds. This was the capstone of 5 months of campus witnessing. Souls were saved and many filled with the Holy Spirit. These students wanted their witness to be public, so they were immersed in the pool. It was like a page out of the Book of Acts.

It didn't happen on a university campus, but along a desert road. An angel of the Lord spoke to Philip the evangelist, who was in Samaria, and told him to go south to the road between Jerusalem and Gaza. When he got there he met a man of some authority, a minister of finance for Candace, the queen of Ethiopia. The man was spiritually hungry, searching, but not finding: He was reading the Book of Isaiah. He invited Philip into his chariot. As they rode along Philip read the Scriptures to the man and explained the good news of Jesus to him. The Ethiopian so completely understood the message that he wanted to show he believed. The Scripture gives us this account:

> And as they went on their way, they came unto a certain water: and the eunuch said, See, here is water; what doth hinder me to be baptized? and Philip said, If thou believest with all thine heart, thou mayest. And he answered and said, I believe that Jesus Christ is the Son of God. And he commanded the chariot to stand still: and they went down both into the water, both Philip and the eunuch; and he baptized him. And when they were come up out of the water, the Spirit of the Lord caught away Philip, that the eunuch saw him no more: and he went on his way rejoicing (Acts 8:36-39).

It's just that simple. Water baptism can take place in a university swimming pool, a pond by the roadside, a river, or a baptistry in a church. The only necessary elements are "belief" and "water."

The university students and the Ethiopian eunuch were saying to whoever might be watching, "I believe." This is the way to let the public know that you believe. The Lord wants the story told by every believer. We believe in the axiom that a picture is worth a thousand words. That is what this picture of baptism is—a thousand words of testimony, a message that spectators can appreciate and understand.

Paul defined the message in Romans 6. He said that those of us who were baptized into Jesus were buried with Him by baptism, and that we were raised up as Christ was raised from the dead to walk in newness of life. There isn't any magic in the water. The act is the picture of what has happened inwardly. The Bible says, "He that believeth and is baptized shall be saved; but he that believeth not shall be damned" (Mark 16:16). It doesn't say he that is not baptized shall be damned. Jesus said, "Thy faith hath saved thee" (Luke 7:50).

Baptism without a change of heart is an empty profession; it is mockery.

## How Much Water Do You Need?

One of the controversies about baptism has been how much water does it take to be baptized? How much water do you think Philip and the eunuch were in? The Bible says, "When they were come up out of the water. . . " The word *baptize* means "to submerge." It is found 74 times in the New Testament. *Baptism* is found 22 times. Not one passage in the Greek New Testament teaches sprinkling as a picture of the gospel of Jesus Christ. Jesus was immersed. John the Baptist "was baptizing in Aenon near to Salim, because there was much water there" (John 3:23).

The believer who comes for Baptism considers himself to be dead to his old life. The old life of sin is left behind, and he purposes to live a new life through the power of Christ's resurrection working in him. This is what the believer is saying by the act of baptism.

## Keep My Commandments

Water baptism is a requirement for every believer. It is a command, not a request. "If ye love me, keep my commandments" (John 14:15). The believer must, out of love and obedience, take immediate steps to be baptized. Such observances as this leave no room for secret discipleship. You will strengthen your entire life and conscience by immediate obedience to this command, "Repent, and be baptized" (Acts 2:38).

# 11

## *Lord, Teach Us To Pray*

> Ask, and it shall be given you; seek, and ye shall find; knock, and it shall be opened unto you (Luke 11:9).

Everybody has exactly the same amount of time to use each day. However, many people complain that they never have enough time. It is difficult to get such people to see the wisdom of planning how to use their time. They are too busy, they say, to take time out just to plan on how to use time. They simply cannot grasp the fact that for every minute spent in planning they can easily save 10 or 15 minutes down the road. They are controlled by what is urgent (although not necessarily important).

Being controlled by the urgent, we shortchange prayer the same way we do planning. We simply can't grasp the fact that we will get more accomplished if we will take time each day to pray.

The real problem is the devil doesn't want any of us to spend time in prayer. So he uses any tactic he can to distract us. He tells us how important it is to do things immediately—we can pray later. He causes all kinds of distractions to rob us of time for prayer.

We would do well to request, as the disciples did, "Lord, teach us to pray.

### Jesus Taught by Example

Actually, Jesus had already begun to teach His disciples to pray—by example. He could have told His disciples the importance of prayer, and how they needed to pray. Instead, He showed them. They saw how often He prayed. It wasn't in so-called spare time that He prayed. It was often after a long, exhausting day of ministering to multitudes of people that Jesus left the crowd and went away to pray.

The disciples had watched Jesus as He healed lepers, opened blinded eyes, and even raised the dead. He was truly unlike any other prophet they knew about. Nevertheless, He found it necessary to find a place to pray.

After Jesus healed a leper, "He withdrew himself into the wilderness, and prayed" (Luke 5:16). Following the healing of a man with a withered hand, "He went out into a mountain to pray, and continued all night in prayer to God" (Luke 6:12). On another occasion, after feeding 5,000, "He was alone praying" (Luke 9:18). And later, "He took Peter and John and James, and went up into a mountain to pray" (Luke 9:28).

Jesus' example was powerful. It said to the disciples that prayer is sometimes more important than sleep or food. Jesus often rose early to pray, and prayed late into and through the night. He prayed in the synagogue, in the wilderness, in the mountains, and in the homes of friends. After Jesus prayed all night in the mountains He served all day in the valley. Jesus prayed in private and in public—the Son of God was a person of prayer.

His prayer life was intensely real. He agonized in prayer until He sweat as it were great drops of blood. His prayer is described in the Book of Hebrews as "supplications with strong crying and tears."

Jesus' example had a positive effect on His disciples. It created in them shame that they had not prayed, and a desire to be able to pray as He prayed.

How can we excuse ourselves for prayerlessness? If

Jesus, the Son of God, needed to take time in His life to pray, how much more we frail human beings need to spend time with our Father in prayer.

Our attempts to pray often seem so feeble in comparison. We stumble along so far short of the example He left for us. We too must cry out, "Lord, teach *us* to pray!"

## Jesus Taught Fundamentals of Prayer

If you have learned to play the piano, speak a foreign language, work mathematical or chemistry problems, you know how essential mastering the fundamentals is. A new piano student cannot play Beethoven's *Moonlight Sonata* after the first three lessons. First comes laborious hours in the fundamentals, until they become automatic reactions.

The great Master Teacher, Jesus, used a model prayer to teach the fundamentals. This prayer is recorded twice in the Gospels—in the Sermon on the Mount (Matthew), and in response to the request from the disciples (Luke).

We know Jesus never intended for this to become a memorized prayer, to be uttered over and over again. He had just criticized the heathen for this kind of empty praying. He very emphatically said, "Don't be like them." Praying is more than going through some form, fingering beads, turning a prayer wheel, or unrolling a prayer mat so many times a day. Prayer is talking with God!

## Principle of Relationship

Too often prayer is totally subjective. It is offered for the alleviation of pain or the acquisition of things in a time of crisis. In praying Jesus said we should first of all admit a relationship: "Our Father, which art in heaven." When you pray, address God as your Father, and place yourself in the receptive position as one of His children.

In other words, prayer should be the natural, expression of a needy child to a loving Father.

What a contrast to the Athenians. When the apostle Paul went to preach to them, he found an altar inscribed, "To the unknown God."

Jesus said, "Pray to your Father in heaven." God is not some vague, distant power, not some pantheistic presence. He is our Father. This prayer isn't for just anyone. Some have pointed out that the Lord's Prayer is really the disciples' prayer. Of course, discipleship is open to "whosoever will."

## Principle of Worship

While we enjoy a close child-father relationship with God, we must always remember that the first purpose of our prayer should be the worship and adoration of God, our Father.

"Hallowed be thy name!" The name of God is to be held high and holy. The prophet Isaiah said that when the seraphim saw the Lord they cried out, "Holy, holy, holy, is the Lord of hosts: the whole earth is full of his glory" (Isaiah 6:3). The effect upon Isaiah was humbling. "Woe is me!" he cried (Isaiah 6:5).

Whether it be in a closet or cathedral, prayer should lift us out of ourselves and beyond our concerns into the holy presence of God, where all of our senses are totally released in worship before His awe-inspiring greatness.

## Principle of Subjection and Submission

It is almost frightening to realize how many times we may have rather halfheartedly, or perhaps even glibly, rattled off, "Thy kingdom come. Thy will be done, as in heaven, so in earth" (Luke 11:2). These words call for total subjection and submission—not so easily given.

The world dominates our lives. We become attached

to possessions; we have a reluctance to renounce them. They appear to be so important, so necessary; at least that's the way we begin to feel. Submitting our wills to God becomes difficult. We must be reminded of His kingdom.

It is dangerous to pray, "Thy will be done." It means you are totally committed to doing whatever God wills for your life. For the apostle Paul it meant a life of travel preaching the gospel, exposure to all sorts of perils, and finally imprisonment and death. Living to do His will means to hold lightly the things of this world, ready to say, do, or go as He leads.

## Principle of Provision

Before we look at the principle of provision, we must look back. So far in this model prayer we have been taught about our relationship to God: "Father," "thy name," "thy kingdom," "thy will."

For the first time we are told to pray subjectively, "Give us." Some take the attitude "God knows who I am and what I need, so whatever comes from day to day is what He wants me to have."

Jesus said to pray for our daily needs: "Give us day by day our daily bread." This principle of trusting God daily to be our provider is difficult at times. We are too prone to look ahead, to store up for the future, to save for a rainy day.

The Israelites learned this lesson of dependence when God sent them bread from heaven. They were told to gather a portion each day. When they gathered more than a day's provision, it spoiled. They learned that God will provide.

God has not changed. He is still our provider. We still need to ask him to provide for us day by day as we walk with Him through life.

This principle of prayer implies a spirit of complete trust and contentment. A trust that says with the songwriter, "I know who holds tomorrow, and I know who holds my hand."

## Principle of Forgiveness

The striking aspect of this principle is the condition upon which it is predicated: "Forgive us as we forgive others!" Now that's putting it right down where we live. My sins are forgiven only to the extent that I am willing to forgive those who have sinned against me.

To be wronged by a fellow human being can be one of the most painful experiences of life. But to allow resentment and bitterness to accrue from the experience can be self-destructive. Booker T. Washington realized this, saying, "I will not permit any man to narrow and degrade my soul by making me hate him."

Jesus didn't say try to understand why someone sinned against you, nor did He encourage us to consider the person or the circumstances. He just said, "Forgive them." On one occasion Peter asked Jesus, "How often should I forgive my brother who sins against me? As many times as seven times?" Jesus' reply was startling, "Seventy times seven!" That didn't mean 490 times. It meant, figuratively speaking, "without number." "If I regard iniquity in my heart, the Lord will not hear me" (Psalm 66:18).

## Principle of Protection

With the present provided for, and the past forgiven, "Lead us not into temptation" assures of protection for the future.

However, this phrase is not easily explained. Why should a child of God have to say to his Father, "Don't expose me to danger"? No normal earthly father would intentionally endanger his child.

We might also ask a question that centers on the word "temptation." The Scriptures say, "Count it all joy when ye fall into divers temptations" (James 1:2). How does this verse in James square with the Lord's prayer for not being led in their direction?

It's not double talk when we say there is temptation and then there is temptation. One is an enticement to do evil; the other offers the possibility of being proved, tested. It is probably the first sense of the word that is meant in the Lord's Prayer.

But what about the idea that God would "lead us" into a situation of evil? The Scriptures say God tempts no man (see James 1:13). On the contrary, He helps us to avoid evil, leading us "in the paths of righteousness for his name's sake" (Psalm 23:3).

There is an interpretation of this petition, based on its verb, that sees "lead into" as "cause not to go." The phrase would then read, "Cause us not to go into temptation." "Do not allow us to be led into temptation."

As the songwriter said, our hearts are "prone to wander." Thus he concluded his song, "Here's my heart, O take and seal it"—another way of saying "lead us not into temptation."

## Principle of Deliverance

While we may be faced with, even harassed with, temptation, there comes a time when we pray, "Lord, deliver us from evil," and He calls a halt to the situation.

Satan would like to see us become discouraged and despondent. The assurance we have is not that God will necessarily change or remove the situation that has brought about the condition. He just delivers us out of the problem.

That's how it was with Job. Satan had vexed him until his whole body was a mass of boils. Even his wife suggested that he curse God and die. But God said Satan had gone far enough. God delivered Job from evil. And Paul spoke with the same assurance: "The Lord shall deliver me from every evil work, and will preserve me unto his heavenly kingdom" (2 Timothy 4:18).

## Jesus Taught the Practice of Prayer

Learning to pray is like learning to walk or talk. The beginner is haltingly frail. The more we pray, the more we learn to pray.

Jesus immediately followed the teachings of His principles in prayer by using a parable to emphasize the practice of prayer. The story is of a man going to a friend to ask a favor, "Lend me three loaves of bread. I have unexpected company and have nothing to set before him." But it was midnight. The man had shut the door, the family was asleep, and it was unreasonable to open the door. Yet the man reasoned, in effect, *Because he is a friend and because of his importunity, I will arise and give him what he wants* (see Luke 11:8).

Jesus did not say the man demonstrated a lack of faith because he continued to ask. On the contrary, Jesus said, ask, seek, knock. Don't give up the first time, or the second time. Dare to be bold. Ask again, seek some more, knock and knock; persistent prayer will get answered.

The story has further significance. The man went at midnight. Don't let the time-consciousness of our day rob you of the answer. Forget about the time, and concentrate on the need and meeting God in prayer.

# 12

## *Giving to God*

> He which soweth sparingly shall reap also sparingly; and he which soweth bountifully shall reap also bountifully (2 Corinthians 9:6).

A few years ago I had the privilege of conducting an interview with the late Dr. Wernher Von Braun, who was considered the foremost rocket engineer in the world. As I waited for his entrance into the conference room, I wondered what kind of a man he would be. Because he was such a brilliant scientist, I concluded that he must be an eccentric who could talk only in scientific vernacular. What a surprise! Without a hint of condescension he conversed in a nonscientific language as he described the wonders of space exploration. During that interview, Dr. Von Braun made a statement that spoke to my heart: "I firmly believe that every man will have to give an account before God as to how he has used the gifts that God has given to him."

Ultimately we will each come face to face with the issue of personal stewardship to God. What have we done with what He has given to us? How have we used the gifts? Have our expenditures of life, time, talents, and money included the work of God?

Throughout the Old Testament, and before, there is evidence that man practiced a principle called tithing, regularly setting aside a tenth of one's income for kingdom purposes. Some Bible students believe that the offerings of Cain and Abel were an allusion to the practice of tithing.

The practice preceded Moses by hundreds of years. History reveals tithing among the ancient Egyptians, Babylonians, and Assyrians.

Abraham tithed, as did Jacob. It was commonly practiced among the Israelites. When and how it began no one knows for sure.

### Holding Out on God

We do know that tithing was used by God among His people. It was an accepted way of life among the Israelites. In fact, the Israelites paid two tithes every year, and a third tithe every third year. They tithed of the produce of their land and their animals. One-tenth of everything was given to the Lord. However, Israel failed to continue tithing. Nehemiah charged them with neglecting their tithes. Furthermore, disregard of their obligation caused Malachi to utter one of the strongest upbraidings given by any of the prophets.

He accused them of robbing God. The people quibbled with him. They could not see any justification for such a stern accusation. But the prophet put his finger on the one thing they were most guilty of. He said, "You have robbed God in tithes and offerings."

### All, Not Some

Apparently the Israelites were guilty more of defrauding than simply forgetting. They imagined that they were satisfying perfectly the requirement of tithing. They were continuing to follow a form, but without a sensitivity for complete obedience. The prophet reminded them again, "Bring ye *all* [not some, not just a token, *all*] the tithes into the storehouse, that there may be meat in mine house, and prove me now herewith, saith the Lord of hosts, if I will not open you the windows of heaven, and pour you out a blessing, that there shall not be room enough to receive it" (Malachi 3:10).

## Cursed With a Curse

The Old Testament record ends on a dismal note. God's people were living in tragic circumstances. Their fields were blighted and their flocks were blemished so that the land groaned beneath the curse. The devourer had gobbled up their crops.

The Israelites' worship was as blighted as their land. They offered polluted bread upon the altar. In fact, they said the table of the Lord was contemptible. Their sacrifices were cast-offs of their flocks—blind, lame, and sick animals.

The Israelites wearied the Lord with their words. They were so twisted in their thinking that they were saying, "Every one that doeth evil is good in the sight of the Lord" (Malachi 2:17).

The devil has many guises for getting around God's truth: He can use the emotional approach and the logical approach with equal ease. He has robbed many people of the blessing of giving by telling them they can't afford to tithe and pay all their bills. And he is right. Often the arithmetic is on his side. If we ignore him, Satan plays on our fears about providing adequately for our families. In all this, one thing Satan causes people to overlook is that nine tenths with God's blessing will go farther than ten tenths without God's blessing. Faith makes it so.

## A Twofold Return

In spite of such flagrant and willful fraud, the Lord was more interested in His people's turning around than in their being cut off. His proposition to them was preceded by one of the greatest promises in the Bible, "For I am the Lord, I change not" (Malachi 3:6). The message was, "Since I don't change, it is obvious that you have. From the days of your fathers you have gone away from My ordinances."

What a gracious proposition He presents, "Return unto me, and I will return unto you" (Malachi 3:7).

Return to God! The Israelites were already God's chosen people. They had not completely turned their backs on God. Even though they didn't bring their best offerings, they did continue to worship Him. That is exactly why the Lord said, "Return unto me." They were paying only token respect. They dropped a few coins in the box as though it were their tithe.

Perhaps their "returning" was not so much to God as to God's ways. By forsaking God's ways the Israelites robbed God. God didn't need the people's tithes, but they needed to give them. They needed the reminder of God's lordship of their lives, which tithing brings, and they needed to learn obedience. The Israelites had known from childhood that God commanded them to tithe, but through carelessness and indifference they decided that God really wouldn't care if they overlooked His command. They didn't hate God. They simply didn't love Him enough. Their delight was not in the Lord or His Law.

## Open the Window, God

Returning to God's ways also means returning to God's blessings.

"Prove me," He said. How? In tithes and offerings. Prove Him by laying aside your tithes and offerings *first* as you receive your income. God can and will bless us, as much as we allow Him to. Too many people want prosperity to precede liberality. God says, "Honor Me first by obedience and cheerful trust, and see if I don't match your liberality with blessings—blessings too great for you to contain."

One day during an early pastorate I answered a rap at the door. As I opened it a man reached out and placed a wad of bills in my hand. He said, "Don't ask my name. I'm not serving God now, but I don't want to owe Him tithes." He turned and left. I never saw or heard from him again. Someone had put the fear of God in him about tithing—if nothing else. Sad to say, the man did not understand that we don't tithe in order to receive God's blessings. Nevertheless, we do know that a faithful God keeps His promises, and that the blessings of God, both spiritual and material, are sure to come as we take God at His Word. Return to God! Return to God's ways! Return to God's blessings!

Today, in this time of grace, some fine Christians contend that although tithing was practiced by the Children of Israel and it was a law under the Old Testament, it has no application to the present.

## Did Jesus Tithe?

By precept and example Jesus taught what the Father expected of His followers. Jesus taught that man must give to live, and that he must lose himself to find himself. Jesus didn't say much about the tithe, nor did He say much about the keeping of the Sabbath. But the Jews in Jesus' day were meticulous in keeping both. It was not necessary for Jesus to say much on either subject, since the Jews were teaching and practicing both religiously.

How many times have you heard someone make the accusation that all preachers can talk about is money. Such a critic would have been uncomfortable under Jesus' ministry. Jesus said a lot about giving and stewardship, but He didn't stop with tithing. Jesus asked for total giving—life, time, talents, and possessions.

Jesus spoke out about tithing on two occasions. The first instance was both a rebuke and an approval of tithing. He chided the scribes and Pharisees, calling them hypocrites because they paid tithes of their spices and omitted weightier matters such as judgment, mercy, and faith. "These you ought to have done, without leaving the others undone" (Matthew 23:23, NKJV). The non-tither comes under the rebuke of the Lord for leaving the tithe unpaid as did the Jews for not doing the "weightier matters." Jesus warned that the righteousness of believers was to "exceed" that of the scribes and Pharisees (Matthew 5:20).

On the other occasion, Jesus was confronted about paying taxes to Caesar. Jesus answered by asking whose "image and superscription" the coins bore. They answered, "Caesar's." Jesus said, "Render to Caesar the things that are Caesar's, and to God the things that are God's." Caesar had a right to the tax. But the tithes belonged to God. There can be little doubt that Jesus paid tithes. Every devout Jew tithed and Jesus was brought up under Jewish training. The Pharisees were constantly watching Jesus so that they could accuse Him of something. Surely they would have used His failure to pay tithes if they could have.

Jesus both practiced and advocated paying tithes. However, He went beyond the tithe. He commended the widow who gave all she had. He asked the rich young ruler to sell all he had and give to the poor. If there is an argument against tithing, it is in the other direction—tithing is a *minimum standard* of giving.

Jesus insisted that everything we have belongs to our Father. The requirement He gave for discipleship is "forsake all and follow me." But He also noted, "Give, and it shall be given unto you; good measure, pressed down, and shaken together, and running over, shall men give into your bosom. For with the same measure that ye mete withal it shall be measured to you again" (Luke 6:38).

The apostle Paul quoted Jesus, "Remember the words of the Lord Jesus, how he said, It is more blessed to give than to receive" (Acts 20:35). Why is this so? How can it be more enjoyable to give than to receive? It can be understood perhaps only by experience. There is true satisfaction in generously giving of yourself and your possessions.

The giving of your offerings to God should not be limited by a set of rules. It should be governed by your love, concern, and compassion. We give back to God as an expression of thanks for the love He has bestowed upon us (see 1 John 4:19).

It is impossible to read the eighth and ninth chapters of 2 Corinthians without realizing Paul had been caught up in the spirit of giving and stewardship that Jesus taught. "First they gave themselves to the Lord" (2 Corinthians 8:5, TEV). Until that is done in all sincerity, no amount of giving will mean anything. When the heart becomes right with God, it will affect our living and our giving. (It would be hard to imagine that the kind of giving Paul talked about was less than the tithe.)

Paul often referred to giving as a grace of God in which believers should abound. He said that the Macedonians, though in poverty, gave liberally. They gave willingly of their substance and of themselves. And their giving added to their joy. Just as Jesus had elevated giving above the law of tithing, so did Paul: "But just as you excel in everything—in faith, in speech, in knowledge, in complete earnestness and in your love for us—see that you also excel in this grace of giving" (2 Corinthians 8:7, NIV).

The "grace of giving" never works a hardship on anyone. Although such giving requires each person to do his best to give liberally and generously, giving should also be proportionate. "It is accepted according to what one has and not according to what he does not have" (2 Corinthians 8:12, NKJV). The tithe is certainly a proportionate measure of giving. But many today have caught the spirit of cheerful giving and are giving far more than 10 percent. The windows of heaven have been opened for them; they are enjoying an overflowing of God's blessings. They are reaping from bountiful sowing; the goodness of God is being measured out to them in direct proportion to how they measured their giving. It is truly "more blessed to give than to receive."

# 13

## *Obedience*

> Thy word have I hid in mine heart, that I might not sin against thee (Psalm 119:11).

A woman who had publicly and privately bemoaned her home and marital plight rehearsed her situation again. Her husband was unsaved and refused to go to church. In fact, he would not even take her to church, and she could not drive a car. She had been raised in a Christian home and had committed her life to the Lord in her youth. She said, "I don't understand why things are this way. I literally prayed for months before marrying him."

My reply to her was a truth she had not accepted, "But you really didn't need to pray at all. The situation was not one of prayer, but obedience." The Word gives explicit instruction about the joining of believers and unbelievers. No amount of prayer can substitute for obedience to the Word. "To obey is better than sacrifice" (1 Samuel 15:22).

### Doers of the Word

Never before have so many copies of the Bible been distributed. Bible societies in the United States and other nations are printing and distributing millions of copies of the Bible each year. The list of translations in modern

English continues to grow. In addition to the printed Word, an assortment of audio cassettes of the entire Bible is available.

We wouldn't want it otherwise. There are still people who do not have a Bible, and God's Word should be available to every person.

Unfortunately, too many people are reading the Bible as just another book. They may be learning intellectually from it, and even be impressed by the truths they read, but it is not enough just to know. We must be doers of the Word.

Throughout the entire Bible, obedience is commanded in man's relationship to God. "Obey my voice, and I will be your God, and ye shall be my people" (Jeremiah 7:23).

## Revival in Israel

In a dark period in Israel's history, God sent along the prophet Nehemiah. Only a remnant of the people was left after their Babylonian captivity and they were in great affliction. When Nehemiah went to Jerusalem he was deeply moved by the walls that lay in rubble and the gates that had been burned. He wept at the scene. He mourned, fasted, and prayed. God used Nehemiah to inspire the people to rebuild the walls in the midst of insurmountable odds. Opposition came from without and discouragement from within.

Israel had been plunged into this deplorable condition because of their disobedience. Finally they listened to God's man, and began to work together.

When the walls were finished, even Israel's enemies confessed that God was with them. It was a time of great healing as the people worked together, "every one unto his work" (Nehemiah 4:15). When at last their tools were put away and they looked at the restored walls, the people rejoiced. The scene that followed resulted in one of the greatest revivals the nation of Israel had ever seen.

## Bring Out the Book

The people of Israel gathered at the wall and called for Ezra the priest to bring out the book of the law of Moses and read to them. They built a great pulpit upon which Ezra stood to read. He began early in the morning and read until noon. As Ezra opened the book the people all stood in reverence. Over 40,000 people had gathered that day.

What mingled emotions were expressed as they heard the Word. They answered Ezra's reading with shouts of Amen! Amen! They lifted their hands, they bowed their heads, they worshiped the Lord with their faces toward the ground. The Israelites wept when they heard the words of the Law. But the day ended in joy as Ezra told them to go their way rejoicing, "for the joy of the Lord is your strength" (Nehemiah 8:10).

## They Obeyed the Word

The days that followed were of greater importance. They were days of prayer, confession, and submission to the Word of the Lord. It took more than weeping over their past failures; the Israelites had to live by the Word that convicted them. Some Bible scholars believe that this revival was the only thing that kept the Children of Israel walking with God through the 400 years of darkness before Christ came. During those years there were no priests worthy to name, no temple in which to worship, no king except one who was corrupt, no prophets giving guidance—only the Word remained with them.

Every great failure in the history of Israel was due to their disobedience. Every great revival was due to obedience, the people's or a leader's. The theme is laced throughout the Bible: *"walk* in the law of the Lord," *"keep* his testimonies," *"walk* in His ways," *"respect* thy statutes," *"keep* thy commandments," *"keep* thy Word," and there are others. If the word *obey* or *obedience* were used in place of these phrases, they would appear hundreds of times throughout the Bible.

## Obedience in Psalm 119

"Wherewithal shall a young man cleanse his way? By taking heed thereunto according to thy word" (Psalm 119:9).

In Psalm 119, David seems to have attempted to capsulize the importance of the Word of God and obedience to it. He used a series of 10 synonyms for the Word: the *Law, testimonies, judgments, statutes, commandments, promise, Word, way, precepts,* and *truth.* Each of these words is used 20 or more times and every verse contains one of them, with the exception of verse 122. The first two verses set the tone of obedience.

> "Blessed are the undefiled in the way,
> who walk in the law of the Lord.
> Blessed are they that keep his testimonies,
> and that seek him with the whole heart"
> (Psalm 119:1,2).

David did not use the word *obey*, but he used many words that connote obedience, such as *walk, keep, respect, taking heed, not wander, meditate, delight,* and many more. No doubt about it, the key note in receiving God's blessings is obedience.

## The Obedience of Jesus

Jesus continued the same emphasis throughout His ministry. His explanation of His own life is wrapped up in these words, "Lo, I come to do thy will, O God" (Hebrews 10:9). He had the same expectation of all who would follow Him; He said no one could enter the Kingdom "but he that doeth the will of my Father which is in heaven" (Matthew 7:21).

For Jesus, obedience was not an act—it was a way of life—and death. He had come into the world for the purpose of pleasing the Father and He gave it all He had.

## He Learned Obedience

While in prison the apostle Paul wrote a letter to the church at Philippi. In his exhortation to them he upheld Christ as their pattern. He said, "Being found in fashion as a man, he humbled himself, and became obedient unto death, even the death of the cross" (Philippians 2:8). The same theme is found again in Hebrews: "Though he were a Son, yet learned he obedience by the things which he suffered" (Hebrews 5:8). Yes, Jesus, the Son of God, learned obedience. His whole life was one of obedience, confining himself, limiting himself, by our human form.

But in the Garden of Gethsemane Jesus learned what obedience was through suffering. His suffering was incomparable. It transcended the common sufferings of humanity. Our Lord's tears in the Garden welled up from a soul exceedingly sorrowful. Being in agony Jesus prayed more earnestly.

In *The Day Christ Died*, Jim Bishop describes Jesus' suffering at the hands of His guards.

> The men [guards] began to enjoy the game. They progressed from slaps to heavy punches on the head and chest and stomach. When Jesus doubled up, they hit Him in the face and that brought Him erect again. They stood close to Him and spat in His face and saw their saliva cling to His cheeks.
>
> Someone in the group had a more amusing idea. He got a cloth and blindfolded Jesus. The guards danced around

Him, cuffing His face and simpering: "Act the prophet, please. Who is it that struck you?" They called Him cruel names. And obscene names. He tired before they did. His knees began to buckle, so they held Him up until He was strong enough to stand alone. Then they beat Him again. (Quoted from *The Day Christ Died [New York: Harper and Row Publishers, Inc., 1978], p. 210.)*

These words tell us why Jesus was obedient, even to death: "He became the author of eternal salvation unto all them that obey him" (Hebrews 5:9). Paul said it another way as he preached to the church at Rome: "By the obedience of one shall many be made righteous" (Romans 5:19). We owe everything to the obedience of Christ.

## How Can We Learn Obedience?

Because of Adam's disobedience, obedience is no longer inherent in human nature. But by virtue of becoming God's child, we have His Spirit in residence. Expecting every child of His to follow Him, God has made it possible once again to respond to Him in obedience, for a part of His Spirit's fruit in our lives is self-control.

"Then said Jesus unto his disciples, If any man will come after me, let him deny himself" (Matthew 16:24).

How did you learn obedience as a child? Often by suffering. It may have come through discipline or the consequences of disobedience. Each of your experiences reinforced the teaching you received on obedience. As you matured, you learned to accept instruction more readily, to give "ear unto wisdom" (Proverbs 2:2).

## Learn the Word

You can't be obedient unless you know what you are to obey. You need to start like the Children of Israel in Jerusalem. Learn the Word. It will affect your life as it did theirs. It pricked their conscience where they were guilty of faulty conduct, and it made them rejoice to know that God was their joy and strength. The Word can make you rejoice too, but if you are unaware of what it says, you surely can't obey it. Start by reading the Word so that you may know what God expects of you.

Jesus said, "Blessed are they that hear the word of God, and keep it" (Luke 11:28). "Keep it" means to obey it. The best place for you to hear the Word is in church. The church was designed in the heart of God to be a place where people could hear His Word. "He gave some, apostles; and some, prophets; and some, evangelists; and some, pastors and teachers; for the perfecting of the saints" (Ephesians 4:11,12).

The best place for you to keep the Word is everywhere: in the home, at the job, on vacation. James said it very plainly, "Be ye doers of the word, and not hearers only, deceiving your own selves" (James 1:22).

## Listen to the Comforter

God knew our frailty and sent the Holy Spirit to help us.

> The Comforter, which is the Holy Ghost, whom the Father will send in my name, he shall teach you all things, and bring all things to your remembrance, whatsoever I have said unto you (John 14:26).

Every time you open your Bible, the Holy Spirit is there to teach you. Listen to Him. Many times we are too caught up in the rush of business as usual. It is easy to shut out the Holy Spirit who is trying to open your mind and heart to the Word. That's His ministry. The Holy Spirit was sent to guide you into all truth.

Even if I had a good memory, I think it would be

impossible to remember everything the Lord says in His Word. Once again the Holy Spirit comes to my aid bringing words and truths back into my consciousness. Why? That I may obey.

A missionary was translating the Bible into a native language. He sought for a word for *obedience* and found none. One day as he was returning from the village, his dog stayed behind. The missionary stopped and gave a loud whistle. Soon the dog came running at top speed. An old native man sitting nearby had observed what had happened and spoke to the missionary in his native tongue. A free translation of what he said was, "Your dog is all ear." At last the missionary had found a beautiful word for obedience. May God help us to be "all ear."

Obedience is not optional. It is a commandment. Otherwise, you deny the Lord Jesus Christ the throne of your life.

> He that hath my commandments, and keepeth them, he it is that loveth me: and he that loveth me shall be loved of my Father, and I will love him, and will manifest myself to him (John 14:21).